DISCLAIMER AND

MW01068723

This book is for informational purposes only and should not be a substitute for advice from a qualified professional. Any information that is offered on this book must be followed at the reader's own discretion. Although the author and publisher have made every effort to ensure that the information in this book was correct at press time, the author and publisher do not assume and hereby disclaim any liability to any party for any loss, damage, or disruption caused by errors or omissions, whether such errors or omissions result from negligence, accident, or any other cause. The advice and strategies contained herein may not be suitable for your situation. Neither the publisher nor author shall be liable for any loss of profit or any other commercial or personal damages, including but not limited to special, incidental, consequential, or other damages.

No part of this publication may be reproduced, distributed, stored in a retrieval system, or transmitted in any form or by any means, including photocopying, recording, or other electronic or mechanical methods, without the prior written permission of the author, except in the case of brief quotations embodied in critical reviews and certain other noncommercial uses permitted by copyright law.

TABLE OF CONTENTS

Section 1: Your Emotions

Section 2: Surviving a Twin Pregnancy

Section 3: Twins and Your Family

Section 4: Preparing Financially for Twins

Section 5: What to Buy

Section 6: Balancing Twins and Work

Section 7: Preparing for a Twin Delivery

Section 8: Caring for Twins

SECTION 1:
YOUR EMOTIONS

HOW TO MANAGE
YOUR EMOTIONS

I was not happy. The minute I saw the two blobs, I knew I was having twins before the doctor even said anything. She and my husband were all smiles. Me? Sure, I had a smile on too… that tried to mask all the emotions I felt on hearing the news.

Because… twins. (Cue freak out moment.)

A chapter on handling your emotions might seem like a strange topic to include in a book about expecting twins, but not only did I want to include this important topic, I wanted to start the book that way.

It's not something we often talk about, but should: how we feel about being parents of twins. Think about this first chapter as a reassuring hug that everything you're feeling is normal.

Emotions you might feel

Fear of…

Not knowing where to start: Beneath the excitement about expecting twins could also be the fear of not knowing where to start. Even if this isn't your first pregnancy, you feel like you're dealing with new territory (maybe even feeling like a first-time mom all over again). If this is your first, then talk about a double whammy. It's easy to feel overwhelmed and not know what to do.

How your body will handle a twin pregnancy: Maybe you're scared about how your body will handle a twin pregnancy. The complications, the larger belly, the extra fatigue. You're scared you're stretching your body to its limits (literally) and how it'll ever bounce back.

Something going wrong in your pregnancy: Twins or otherwise, we all have fears about something going wrong during pregnancy. Having twins doesn't help with the fear, either. With extra complications, you might be afraid of every little thing that could go wrong.

Worry about...

How you'll ever afford twins: Whether you feel like your finances are "just right" or you're barely scraping by as it is, finances are one of the biggest worries on twin parents' minds. With twins in the mix, maybe you're worried about how you'll ever afford childcare or hospital bills or even day-to-day purchases.

Your other kids: Maybe you already have an older child (or more) and you're worried about how he'll react to having two baby siblings. Will he regress, or act up? Will he feel hurt with having less of your attention? How will you manage caring for him and two newborns?

Anxiety about...

The extra attention: With twins come the inevitable extra attention you'll get, and sometimes you may not like the many questions and comments, or that your loved ones will be making a big deal about welcoming twins into the family. You might have a friend whose jaw drops when you tell her you have twins, or coworkers who can't hide their reactions.

The technicalities: Where will they sleep? How will we fit three car seats in the car? What do we do about childcare? Your mind is probably moving so fast with all the possible scenarios you feel like you need to solve. It feels overwhelming thinking about all the details you now have to think about from being a mom of twins.

Guilt because...

You feel unhappy: A part of you likes the idea of having twins... and another part dreads the thought of it. It's that dread that might make you feel guilty. Even ungrateful. *Shouldn't I feel happy?* You might think. *Especially when others struggle to conceive even just one?*

You might even feel guilty because others around you are so enthusiastic about the news of twins. Meanwhile, you're barely able to catch your breath from all the other emotions that seem to weigh you down.

You can't spend one-on-one time with your twins: A big concern among twin moms is the guilt they feel for not spending one-on-one time. We imagine or have experienced caring for a singleton and all the attention we give them. With twins, it seems impossible to set aside time to bond with each one (spoiler alert: it's totally possible).

This is just a snippet of the many emotions you might be feeling. You'll likely feel them come and go in waves, so that

one day you're super excited about picking out names,
then the next, you're wondering how you'll ever afford caring
for twins.

I wanted to begin the book with this chapter because this is
the start of your journey. We'll address each of these emotions
and concerns so you'll feel better prepared for what's to come.
I hope that, after going through the book, you'll feel more
confident, less scared, and more knowledgeable about the world
of twins.

But what about right this moment? What can you do? Here's
what I learned: where you are now is still so far away from when
your twins will be born. Everything seems overwhelming when
you're staring at the finish line from the starting line. When you
have a long list of things you still haven't done but somehow
have to complete before the twins arrive.

My advice? Take action on only the things you can do within
the next three months, at the most. Yes, have big-picture goals,
such as saving for a new van or thinking about maternity leave,
but don't plan to do anything tangible with anything you can't
do anything about within the next three months.

Try not to get too ahead of planning and take action on only the
things you can do within the next three months. Break down
your goals and tasks by the month, then write specific tasks
on the weekly planners. Focusing on actionable items you can
actually do instead of worrying about what you can't will feel
more productive.

Will the overwhelming emotions ever go away? Yes, especially
as you get used to your new role. You may have just found out

about twins and are still getting used to the idea. Maybe it still feels surreal, or the emotions bounce back and forth.

The first few weeks after hearing the news can be pretty intense, but over the next few weeks and months, you'll adjust and get used to the idea of carrying twins. You'll slowly piece together plans about childcare and sleeping arrangements. Your finances will seem more doable, and things will make more sense.

For now, know that you're not alone, no matter how it feels that way sometimes. That it's okay to feel whatever it is you're going through, from joy to sadness to anxiety. This doesn't make you a bad mom, but rather an honest one who can accept her emotions in a healthy way.

Find positive reinforcement

Even from well-meaning friends and family, I still cringed at some of their comments or reactions. Sometimes it was the pity written on their face, as if I had just stumbled on the worst luck. With others, it was the worry about how to handle it all, and sometimes even the over-excitement was enough to overwhelm me.

If you find yourself surrounded by reactions and emotions you're not comfortable with from others, find it in other places. The best places are other twin moms going through or having gone through the same thing. You can find a moms of multiples group for meet ups, or online twin forums.

This is actually one of the reasons I started our Facebook group, All About Twins, to help foster the support and encouragement I knew twin parents needed. Not just through the pregnancy, but for the months and years down the line.

It's important to surround yourself with positive reinforcement. People who will listen to your changing moods without judgment, or support you through the tough days.

It'll be alright

It's hard to see this right now, but not only are your emotions normal and real, they'll also ebb and flow with time.

Yes, you'll be in survival mode the first three or so months. When you're in this stage, accept that life is different, but that, in many ways, it's also temporary. Your twins will grow up, sleep well, and you'll be able to return to your routine, but don't rush to that stage. Instead, accept this stage and know that it won't last forever.

You'll also find that once you have your twins, it's not as daunting as it seems. All the nightmares and the crazy end-of-pregnancy scenarios likely didn't happen, or at least not as intensely as you imagined.

You'll meet your fears head-on in the best way I know how: by simply doing it. I was scared to take my twins out alone, but when you force yourself to do it (or have no other choice), you'll feel stronger and more empowered to tackle it again.

Start small, maybe with a quick stroll around the block. Then work yourself up to higher levels of challenges, and you'll arrive feeling tired and exhausted but accomplished. This is how we deal with our fears and jitters: by meeting them head on.

HOW TO STAY POSITIVE

Double the fatigue and nausea. Struggling to gain enough weight. Pregnancy complications. Your preschooler acting up just when you least need him to. Catching a cold... five times during your pregnancy.

A twin pregnancy is a challenging experience, and your twins haven't even arrived yet! You're just about ready to throw in the towel because the days feel so hard to get through.

How can you stay positive when times are tough?

Look for the good

Even when everything seems to be going wrong, you can always find goodness around you. Simple things like your babies' health, or being in the hands of competent doctors. Drinking a delicious smoothie or your child kissing your belly.

These may be small or overlooked positives, but added up, they remind you of the good things you have, even in the face of overwhelming challenges.

Look for solutions

Be proactive about possible solutions you can find. If complications are taking a toll on you, learn from your doctor all the ways to best cope with it. If money problems are keeping you up at night, develop a budget to see where you can go from here.

Not every problem has a clear solution in front of it, but your time is better spent thinking about things you can do.

Find distractions

It's too easy to brood over our misfortunes. Finding distractions shifts the focus elsewhere. Watch a funny show, read a book, or play games on your smart phone. Talk to family and friends about other things besides the challenges of a twin pregnancy. Even if distractions only work for a few minutes at a time, they can be all you need to change your mindset.

Talk, cry, and vent

Don't bottle up all your emotions and frustrations. Talk about it with your partner. Cry, whether to someone else or on your own. Vent with other twin moms who can understand what you're going through.

Getting your words out into the open restores the chaos in your mind. Sharing your emotions makes them feel not so overwhelming.

Remember what it's all for

When times feel too tough to keep going, remember your goals. Remember that every day your twins are in your belly are less days they're in the hospital. Remember that this is temporary, even when weeks and days feel like forever.

You'll cry and get frustrated during this twin pregnancy, but you'll realize you still have good things in your life. That this is temporary, and that you have an amazing family—with two little ones on the way—worth holding on for.

SECTION 2:
SURVIVING A TWIN PREGNANCY

TYPES OF TWINS AND
TWIN PREGNANCIES

Like many moms, your biggest concern is likely a safe and healthy pregnancy. I don't blame you: twin pregnancies tend to have more complications than singleton ones. They're more uncomfortable and need frequent monitoring, and it seems you're introduced to a whole new lingo of what exactly a twin pregnancy is all about.

Identical vs fraternal

Twins fall into two categories: identical or fraternal. Identical twins form when a mother's fertilized egg divides into two. Fraternal twins occur when two sperm fertilize two separate eggs.

Boy-girl twins are always fraternal. Same-gendered twins can be either identical or fraternal.

Identical twins

The best way to confirm whether your twins are identical or fraternal is through a DNA test. You can order lab kits and swipe the inside cheeks of your twins to see if they do in fact share the same DNA.

Even though identical twins share the same DNA, they don't always look alike. Birth position, formation in the womb, and environment can make them look different. Think of identical twins' DNA as an architect's blueprint for two homes. The blueprints may look the same, but small differences can happen during construction.

Fraternal twins

Fraternal twins form from two sperm and two eggs, so they always have different DNA. Think of fraternal twins as any other sibling pair, just growing in the womb at the same time.

Genetics can lead to a likelihood of having fraternal twins through the mother's side (some women have a higher chance of dropping more than one egg at a time during ovulation). Age also plays a factor—older women tend to drop more than one egg, and in vitro fertilization also contributes to fraternal twins.

DiDi / MoDi / MoMo

If your head just spun looking at that title, don't worry: we'll break it down. Those are all abbreviations for the different ways twins form in the womb.

DiDi

DiDi stands for Dichorionic-Diamniotic and happens when:

- the twins are fraternal (two sperm fertilize two eggs), or
- a single fertilized egg is divided by the third day after fertilization

DiDi twins are usually fraternal, but in a few cases (like splitting by the third day) can also be identical. DiDi twins have two separate amniotic sacs and two separate placentas.

MoDi

MoDi stands for Monochorionic-Diamniotic. This happens when a single cell divides four to eight days after fertilization. They're almost always identical.

MoDi twins share the same placenta but live in their own amniotic sacs.

MoMo

MoMo stands for Monochorionic-Monoamniotic. This happens when a single cell divides nine days after fertilization. They're always identical.

MoMo twins not only share the same placenta like MoDi twins, they also live in the same amniotic sac.

Baby A and Baby B

Did you notice that your doctor referred to your twins as Baby A and Baby B? Your doctors will track your twins as either A or B. This helps them see how each baby is growing. How do they know which one is A or B? Baby A is the one closest to cervix.

If all this sounds overwhelming, take a deep breath. Knowing the type of twins you have will help your doctor better check your pregnancy. Prenatal care is your best bet to having a safe and healthy pregnancy and delivery.

WHAT TO KNOW ABOUT
A TWIN PREGNANCY

I thought I had pregnancy down pat with my singleton. I did the research and went through nine months of pregnancy and finally, delivery. I figured my second pregnancy would be as simple as the first time around.

Then, when I found out about the twins, I felt like I entered a whole new world with requirements and protocols I didn't need to know with a singleton.

What you need to know about a twin pregnancy

Important: This book is for informational purposes only. Always discuss with your doctor your own personal medical needs.

How much weight to gain

As you might have guessed, carrying twins means you'll gain more weight. You're carrying two babies, pumping more blood and hormones, and likely two placentas. A typical twin mom should gain about 35 to 45 pounds by the end of her pregnancy. We all have different body types and needs. Ask your doctor how much weight you need to gain for a healthy twin pregnancy.

The first trimester can be difficult to gain weight with morning sickness, but the general rule is to gain 24 pounds by week 24. Hopefully you'll have less nausea the second trimester and gain enough weight then. Your main goal is to consume enough calories to grow your babies.

How to gain enough weight

Although any calories is better than no calories, try to stay away from unhealthy food. A diet of burgers and shakes can lead to complications down the line (trust me, I know!).

Instead, you can try to:

- **Drink your meals through smoothies or juices.** Rather than chewing platefuls of vegetables, blend or juice them into smoothies. You'll consume healthy calories quickly and easily.

- **Eat high-protein healthy food.** Things like avocados, nuts, and eggs.

- **Drink protein shakes or bars.** You'll add calories as supplements to your regular meals.

Because you're carrying twins, you want to consume an extra 600 calories a day. Factor in how many calories you eat on a regular day, then add in an extra 600 calories, or to keep it simple, watch your scale to gauge whether you're on the right track.

Morning sickness

Most moms experience morning sickness during the first 13 weeks of their pregnancy. You might feel nauseous and fatigued.

Food might repulse you, even those you may once have enjoyed.

So, how can you cope with this ongoing feeling?

- **Eat small servings throughout the day.** Rather than sitting down for three large meals, spread them out over several hours. Your stomach won't feel so full after each meal.

- **Eat bland food.** Follow your food preferences and stay away from anything that grosses you out. You'll have better luck with food like crackers, applesauce, yogurt, fruits, baked and grilled meats, peanut butter, bread, cereal, oatmeal, and potatoes.

- **Drink lemon and ginger tea.** Many moms swear by drinking lemon and ginger to reduce morning sickness discomfort.

- **Move slowly.** Morning sickness includes nausea and dizziness. Avoid moving quickly, such as standing right away or walking fast.

- **Rest!** The mantra of a twin pregnancy, rest is important and effective with morning sickness. The more you can rest, the better.

HOW TO HAVE A HEALTHY
TWIN PREGNANCY

We all want to carry our twins as long as possible and avoid complications. Nothing guarantees a complication-free pregnancy, but you can establish healthy habits to increase the chances.

These are the three areas pregnant twin moms need to focus on:

- Rest
- Eat well
- Drink water

Rest

As you may have noticed even before you learned about your twins, morning sickness is stronger with twins. You're likely making two placentas, which doubles your morning sickness symptoms and hormones.

You're also carrying two babies, two placentas, and double the blood and hormones. The extra weight takes its toll earlier than if you were carrying one. You might see singleton pregnant women carrying on with their routine up to eight months. Meanwhile, you're already exhausted even without a twin belly showing yet.

To drive the point home: a twin pregnancy at 32 weeks is equal to a singleton pregnancy at 40 weeks. Don't feel like you're exaggerating when you say you're tired or have morning sickness. They're real and common among twin moms.

While it might seem unrealistic for you to rest often, you need to listen to your body. Let's look at different ways you can get the rest you need during your twin pregnancy.

Don't exercise as much

Don't exercise as much as you're used to. Exercise in a twin pregnancy isn't as important as it is for a singleton one. Avoid pushing your body beyond its limits.

Consider your previous activity level. A mom who exercised five days a week will have different needs than another who didn't work out. The best way to incorporate exercise if need be is to change your former workouts to a lower intensity. Always check with your doctor about your physical activity.

While you don't need to exercise, you also shouldn't be a sloth, either. Unless your doctor advises absolute bed rest, do try to move around. Being in the same position will feel more uncomfortable than moving your body.

Sleep

As you near your third trimester, sleep becomes even more challenging. You're bigger and won't be able to sleep on your back any longer, and you might have complications like I did that keep you up all night.

Take advantage of whatever sleep you can gather while you can. If you're sleepy at night, don't push yourself to stay up longer to finish a task or to read another chapter. If you have a chance, take a nap during the day. Sleeping does so many wonders during a twin pregnancy.

Reduce chores

Our tasks never seem to end. You might even think it impossible to leave all your tasks undone just so you can rest, but question whether each task is important, and if you can find an alternative.

For instance, instead of washing dishes, can you use disposable plates and utensils? Instead of cooking, can you order a meal? Instead of deep cleaning your home, can you hire a cleaning service to do a big sweep (or simply leave it undone)?

For the absolute essentials, can you ask someone else to do it for you? Can you vacuum weekly instead of daily?

As difficult as it is to let go of your routine, sometimes we have to admit we're in a different season in our lives. Just like all seasons, they come and go. You won't always order in or have a messy home, but accepting that it is what it is for now will take the pressure off from maintaining your usual lifestyle.

Limit travel

A mom carrying one baby can usually travel up to 34 to 36 weeks, but a mom carrying twins isn't supposed to travel past 24 weeks.

For many twin moms, 24 weeks and beyond is survival mode. You're likely more uncomfortable than in the past. Traveling is already exhausting even for a regular, non-pregnant person. Adding a twin pregnancy at this stage will be even more of a challenge.

At 24 weeks, babies are also more viable to survive outside the womb. Should you need to deliver, they'd need to admit your twins to the nearest NICU. They wouldn't be released until they're ready to go home. If you're traveling, this can be complicated to deal with.

Explain your condition to your family

A twin pregnancy not only takes its toll on mom, but on the rest of the family as well. Think of your twin pregnancy as a family affair (with you doing the important work!). Every person in the family has to pitch in and understand that things will be different sometimes.

For those with young children, this can be especially difficult to communicate. How do you tell your toddler you can't walk around the block anymore? Or that he has to play with his trains while you talk to him from the couch? It's hard to imagine, and definitely a struggle for everyone involved.

Still, try to find new and creative ways to be with your family. Focus on light activities to do with your young children. Ask your older ones to take care of their own dishes or laundry. Explain to your partner how you can only do so much around the house and will need his help with everything else.

I know how difficult it can be to lay on the couch while so much needs to get done. How hard it is to watch your partner do all the chores while you seem to be doing nothing but lying down. But don't think of it that way. You're doing so much by making those babies and keeping them in as long as possible. You're avoiding complications that could make things much worse if you pushed yourself.

Eat well

Eating well is another key factor in increasing your chances of a healthy twin pregnancy.

Consume enough calories

During a twin pregnancy, you'll want to gain 24 pounds by week 24. This might change depending on your unique physical needs. Always ask your doctor whether this rule of thumb applies to you, but in most cases, you want to gain that amount within that time frame.

With that goal, you'd be gaining a pound a week, assuming you gain any during the first trimester. I was so nauseous the first trimester, I gained a measly two pounds in all those 13 weeks.

Still, do your best to consume as many calories as you can. Find the foods you enjoy and can consume. Drink smoothies and juices so consuming calories is quicker than chewing platefuls of meals, and add protein supplements or eat protein bars for extra calories to your meals.

Eat healthy food

Although any calories is better than no calories, do your best to eat healthy food. I made the mistake of eating rich and fatty foods, desperate to gain those 24 pounds. While I'm glad I gained that weight, I wish I had eaten healthier options instead.

Drink smoothies and juices so you're consuming the same amount of calories in a drink. Choose high-protein and food with healthy fat, like avocados, eggs, yogurt, and lean meats, and avoid empty calories or rich sweets.

Extra vitamins

With a singleton pregnancy, one prenatal vitamin was enough to get you through the day. With a twin pregnancy, you'll likely need more than that. In my case, my doctor prescribed 2,000 IU of vitamin D and 1,000 mg of calcium on top of my regular prenatal vitamin. (For comparison's sake, a typical prenatal vitamin only has 220 IU of vitamin D and 145 mg of calcium.)

You'll likely also need an iron supplement to accommodate the extra blood you're producing, and your doctor will probably make sure you take at least 1mg of folic acid.

These vitamins make sure your body is in its best condition and has the nutrients to produce two babies. Food offers many of these nutrients, but your body will need more than you can consume just through food.

Drink a lot of water

I always considered myself a big water drinker. I don't drink anything else, other than tea. So when I heard the advice that I should drink one gallon—or 16 (8-ounce) cups—of water per day, I assumed I had been doing this. Just to be safe though, I began measuring and tracking how many cups I drank for the day.

So imagine my surprise when I only reached 10 cups, and that's with me putting in effort. Staying hydrated helps to prevent contractions. This is why we're often told to drink water when we feel Braxton Hicks contractions, and why drinking water is important to maintaining a healthy and clean body.

Bring either a gallon or half gallon (a 64-ounce) cup with you everywhere. Then you'll know whether you met your goal for the day when you've emptied the container. Keep your cup near your desk or wherever you're located.

Having a healthy and safe pregnancy is top priority for twin moms. Unfortunately, it's not something we can always control. Different circumstances, physical needs, or "it just happens" well... happens.

Still, focus on things you know will likely help you during your pregnancy. Rest as much as you can because your body is doing a ton of work inside. Eat enough calories to gain weight, focusing on healthy meals, and drink a gallon of water a day to give your body the hydration it needs. A twin pregnancy is difficult, but with the right framework, can be safe and healthy through delivery.

SECTION 3:
TWINS AND YOUR FAMILY

PREPARING YOUR CHILD
FOR TWINS

Adjusting to the news about twins was already a challenge
enough. Now it's time to prepare the rest of your family. Maybe
you're worried about how your older children will handle
welcoming two babies, or you're wondering how you'll nurse the
twins and still tend to your four-year-old.

When I began writing this guide, I thought I'd have a little blip
about how to handle your other children. After all, not everyone
has other children when they're expecting twins, but so many
people voiced their worries about their other children I knew I
needed to talk a lot about it.

Preparing your child for twins

If you've ever felt apprehensive about introducing twins to your
older child, you're not alone. I remember seeing my then-three-
year-old's smiling face and thinking, *You have no idea what's
about to happen.*

It's tough for kids to adjust to one baby, let alone two. He won't
spend as much time with you like he does now. You'll feel more
tired and be more likely to snap and lose your patience, and a
more attention will go toward the two babies.

But starting now, you can begin to prepare him for what's to come. While he won't understand the changes yet, he'll feel better informed when they do.

Set the scene and establish expectations

Around the time you begin to show, explain to your child you're about to have two babies in a few months. Project the positives of having siblings, such as holding them or having future playmates. Mention any new babies he may have met for better reference ("Remember how we visited Aunt Samantha and we saw her baby?").

As you explain the exciting changes about to happen, glorify his new role as a big brother. Praise him when he behaves or takes care of his toys (or even you!), and talk about how much he can "teach" his new siblings, highlighting all the things he can do that they can't yet. Stuff like being able to play with toys, eating a meal on his own, or getting dressed.

At the same time, share examples of what he can expect with newborn twins. Describe a reality he can understand at his age. For instance, tell him that:

- **Babies cry to tell us what they need.** It's also good to point out that they're not always distressed when they cry. If he assumes every cry means they're upset, he might grow anxious if they don't stop crying immediately. Instead, say, "Let's see what they want," or "What do you think he's trying to tell us?"

- **You'll be busy with the babies.** There might be times when he asks for something and he might have to wait. Assure him you'll get to him first if possible, but sometimes the babies might need you as well.

- **You'll have visitors.** Let him know that your house might be full with visitors who want to play with him and meet the new babies.

- **It's good to play independently.** Over the course of your pregnancy, you won't be able to be with him in ways he's used to. You could be too tired to sit up from the couch, much less play at the park. Give him opportunities to play alone, even with you sitting nearby. He'll know what to do with himself if you're busy with the twins.

Transition your child into new milestones

Along with newborn twins are the inevitable transitions your older child will go through. For instance, moving him to a regular bed so you can use his old crib. Many kids are "moved out" of their current set-up to make space for their twin siblings. These changes can include sleeping in a new room or forgoing a highchair for his younger siblings.

Any time you transition your older child, don't "blame" it on the twins. Tell him he's moving to a big bed so he's more comfortable (not because you need his crib), or say you can't roughhouse because you're tired (not because you're carrying the twins).

Avoid blaming the twins for changes in his life so he doesn't resent them. Instead, phrase the changes as exciting and expected transitions.

What about your child's developmental milestones, such as potty training? It's tempting to push them towards milestones to make caring for twins easier, but follow your child's lead. Introduce the concept and begin preparing him for potty use, but don't force it on him if he's not ready.

Bring consistency into your child's life

With so many changes about to happen, consistency is key in your child's life. Consistency and routine give him structure to balance the chaos at home. They're familiar standbys to rely on and feel comforting when everything else seems crazy.

As much as possible, maintain your current routine. Keep bedtime and naps the same, as well as when he expects to eat and play. Stick to your same bedtime routine of taking a bath, singing, and reading books. These little actions remind him he still has a place at home.

And consider introducing other routines into his life before the twins arrive. Maybe enroll him in preschool, or begin a tradition of Fridays with Grandma. Give him a space that's all his own that isn't baby-related. A place he can escape to and rely on.

Preparing your child for twins begins now. Set expectations early and at a level he can understand. Highlight the positives of having twins, but give him age-appropriate expectations as well. Transition him into new milestones without "blaming" the twins for these changes, and build consistency and regularity into his life so he has a familiar routine to rely on.

HANDLING YOUR
CHILD'S BEHAVIOR

Tantrums. Defiance. Whining. Whether during pregnancy or after the twins are home, your child's behavior can be a challenge.

If you're overwhelmed with twins, you can imagine how he feels about it. He's going through so many emotions and adjusting to change that he behaves in the only ways he knows how. Young children can't communicate in ways you and I can. They don't understand this is temporary, that they still have a place in the family or that you still love them.

So they act up. They throw tantrums or make unreasonable demands. They regress into previous behaviors (perhaps even to mimic his baby siblings). They'll test your patience at the most inconvenient of times.

No matter how annoying or frustrating this may be, know that it's normal. Even the most excited big brother or big sister will exhibit behavior issues at some point, and even the most patient parent is bound to lose her temper. Let's take a look at three common issues you might see:

Regression

Many children four and younger can't grasp the concept of a new sibling as well as older children, and they're more overwhelmed about the new changes that twins bring.

They're also experiencing their own developmental changes. These factors make children the most likely to regress and "undo" their past accomplishments. Let's review a few:

- **Speech:** Your older child starts talking in "baby talk."

- **Whining and tantrums:** He resumes the temper tantrums and whining you thought were long gone by now.

- **Sleep:** No longer sleeping through the night, he'll wake more frequently as he tries to understand his feelings.

- **Using the potty:** Seeing his parents change diapers makes him crave the one-on-one attention of diaper changes. He may also be distracted and have more accidents.

- **Feeding:** He may ask to nurse or have a bottle when he sees the twins doing the same.

So, how do you deal with your older child's regression?

Don't scold or lecture

Avoid lecturing him. Regression is normal, even expected. Expressing your disappointment will only make him feel worse about himself and the situation.

Show empathy

Instead, honor the intentions and show empathy. Let him know you understand why he's feeling that way. You might say, "It's pretty easy to forget to use the potty, especially with all the new things going on."

Don't enable old habits

While you shouldn't lecture him on using a pacifier, you shouldn't allow him to keep doing so, either. For certain regressions, don't encourage him or assume these habits help him feel better. Instead...

Spend quality time together

All these regressions are your child's cry for help. Find any opportunity you can to spend alone time with him. You might ask, "What do you want to do now?"

He'll love that you give him attention the second you have a chance to. He'll be able to do activities he used to do with you. Plus, those special moments are opportunities for him to share his apprehensions and fears.

Foster a close relationship with his siblings

Remember how I mentioned "blaming" the twins? Your older child might resent the twins if he feels like they're the reason for his misery. Foster a close relationship among them instead.

Let's say you're all playing with the twins and they're reaching their arms out at him. Tell him, "Look—he wants to give you a hug!" Or have him hold out his finger for the babies to grasp. Encourage him to delight in his new siblings and explain they're now one big group.

Attachment

Does your older child prefer you over other adults? Managing his behavior is more difficult when he's attached and prefers you over others. Through pregnancy and the twins' arrival, you'll be less available to be with him, as much as you'd like to. This might make him feel threatened and set off behavior issues you'd rather not deal with.

What to do?

Begin encouraging his attachments with other adults. Even if he protests and wants you, have his dad carry him instead. Schedule special outings with just him and your partner, or ask Grandma if he can sleep over for the weekend. Sneak away for a few hours so he's able to spend time with others.

As you encourage attachment to other adults, spend quality time with him, being completely present and focused on him.

Surround him with family and friends too so he's used to being in the company of other people. Invite your friend and her family over for dinner. Attend play dates. Do little things to remind him he has a village to rely on besides you.

Of course nothing will replace you, but he'll have to spend time with others while you're busy. Starting now won't feel so much of a shock when that happens.

Managing your temper

Your child isn't the only one who might find herself struggling to behave. What happens if *you're* the one unable to cope with your temper, or whose patience wanes from the toll of sleep deprivation?

Losing your temper can happen early, even while you're still pregnant with the twins. Those last weeks in particular can be difficult for many twin moms. We're tired beyond belief, we're cross, and we snap.

Or your temper might escalate once your twins arrive and you're sleep-deprived. Maybe you're battling through emotions you never knew you had.

I noticed a lapse in anger management around the last few weeks of my pregnancy and when the twins arrived. I found myself getting angry, followed by the guilt at what I'd just said or done.

How do you cope with frustration and not lose your temper with your older child?

Find your triggers

We react to cues and triggers that set us off, sometimes unaware we've reacted until it's too late. Often we don't even realize what we've reacted to.

You might think you're reacting to your child's whining, or because he isn't listening again, but over time, you'll notice patterns. So the next time you yell, think about what triggered your reaction.

It could be when your child whines in that high-pitched voice, or keeps asking the same question over and over, or does something you just told him not to do that sends you boiling.

You'll have different triggers, and your task is to find the common ones that set you off. By being aware of these triggers, you're putting a stop between the cue and your reaction. Instead of yelling immediately after he whines, you spot the whining first. This is important because after you spot your triggers, you'll need to...

Pause

Once you've spotted your trigger, you've given space between it and your reaction. This space—this pause—stops you from yelling. It gives you an opportunity to redirect your emotions.

You're not going to erase your frustration when you pause for that one second, but you *will* be able to stop yourself from yelling and do something else.

Maybe that's taking a breath instead of saying something you might regret, or walking away to collect yourself. Even saying your trigger out loud ("He's whining") can be enough to change course. You'll still have heightened emotions, but they'll be less likely to make you lose your temper.

Ignore or walk away

Yes, it's fine for you to walk away or ignore your child to keep you from getting angry. Let him know you're angry right now and need five minutes to be alone to calm back down to normal.

Sometimes we feel compelled to "fix" the problem right then and there. Except we don't resolve anything in a healthy way when we're still heated with emotion.

Instead, walk away and collect yourself. There's no rule saying you need to sit down with your child and resolve the issue at that moment. Sometimes I'll wait as long as the next day before addressing an issue. It's better to communicate when you've calmed down, even if it means walking away for a few minutes.

Apologize

If you find yourself yelling or losing your temper with your child, always apologize. You can't undo words or actions, but you *can* express remorse.

Apologizing respects children. They're human beings we need to value and make amends with, just as we would another adult.

Apologizing also humbles us. Our mistakes remind us we're always learning and improving. We remember we're also changing and growing just as we'd hope our kids would.

Don't beat yourself up over it

While every mistake is a learning opportunity, it's useless to let your guilt consume you. You're not perfect, nor will you ever be—and that's okay. This isn't a cop-out inviting you to lose your temper and not feel remorse. Rather, it's a reminder for how better you'll be learning from the moment, and moving on.

We all have different thresholds for losing our tempers, and sometimes they come in seasons. I yelled at my eldest twice in all his first three years, but once the twins arrived, it had grown into a daily problem I needed to resolve.

Finding your triggers, pausing, and redirecting your response elsewhere make a huge difference. When you *do* lose your temper, forgive yourself and move on—it's what your older child needs you to do most.

As you can see, preparing your child for twins can be a challenge. He might regress or misbehave more than usual. You might lose your temper, and he might feel displaced or shocked at not having you all to himself, especially if he feels attached. By applying these lessons, you can ease the brunt of it and prepare him as best as possible for his siblings.

Behavior aside, you're in a unique position: how do you balance all your children's needs? Whether you already have an older child or will need to juggle your twins, the next chapter shares how to balance all your children's needs.

BALANCING ALL YOUR
CHILDREN'S NEEDS

We've talked about preparing your child for twins as well as how to manage his behavior. In this chapter, we'll learn how to balance his needs with those of the twins.

When they all need you at the same time

Imagine you've settled into your nursing position when your child says he needs to use the potty, or you're rocking one twin to sleep when he climbs up next to you wanting to play. For many twin moms, this is the nightmare they hope to never face.

Unfortunately, it happens all too often. In the early days, have another adult with you for an extra set of hands.

But what do you do when that person goes back to work or flies home after staying with you for a few weeks? You're alone with your twins and your older child—three of them and only one of you.

Tend to your older child first

First, take a deep breath... because there IS only one of you. You can't do everything, and that's okay.

Second, as much as possible, tend to your older child first. Yes, even if the twins are crying. Don't assume you always need to go to the twins first just because they're babies.

When more than one child needs you, make it a point to ask yourself, *Can I tend to my older child first?* You might be surprised at how many opportunities you have to meet his needs before the twins'. Using your best judgment and see if you can attend to him first. Maybe he wants help arranging his cars, and it's only going to take a few seconds to do.

Using the potty

What to do about potty use, particularly if you're busy nursing or feeding the twins and can't jump up and run to him?

Forcing potty training to meet a deadline (such as being potty trained by the time the twins arrive) won't work. Even if you use a quick potty training method, that can only be successful if he's actually ready to potty train.

Let's say he's ready to potty train. Don't start too close to when the twins arrive. You're better off waiting several weeks after they're home than starting too close. He's already going through so many changes with the twins—he doesn't need yet another one to grapple with.

Okay, so let's say he's potty trained, but still needs help with using the potty. He may need help pulling his pants down, or wiping his butt if he poops. Here are tips on how to manage:

- **Get a floor potty seat he can easily sit and stand from.** You avoid having to carry him onto the big toilet, even if it has a potty-sized seat on top.

- **Put him in elastic and easy-to-remove shorts or pants.** Then begin encouraging him to pull them down and up on his own.

- **Before you begin a feeding session, take him to the potty.**

- **Leave books near the potty.** Explain that if he poops and you're still busy, he should keep sitting and read books until you come to wipe him.

- **If you anticipate problems, put him in training pants.**

- **Don't worry about accidents**—you can always clean them up later.

Nursing or feeding

It's tough feeling tied to your twins while nursing, pumping, or holding two bottles. You can't exactly stand up right away if your older child needs you. What to do?

- **Encourage independent play.** Before you welcome your twins, encourage your older child to feel comfortable playing alone. He'll have more opportunities to lead his own play without adult distractions.

- **Gather new toys and items he can tinker with while you're busy.** These can be simple dollar toys or even household items. Then when it's time to nurse, introduce these new items to keep him busy.

- **Give him tasks to do.** Encourage him to fill his big brother role by asking for his help. Things like putting diapers in the diaper box, sorting socks, or putting toys away.

- **Read with him.** Sit next to him and have him turn the pages of a book while you read the words aloud.

- **Give him a time frame.** Your child may just need the reassurance that you'll be with him soon. Explain that you'll be able to play trucks with him in 15 minutes.

- **Ask him to entertain the babies.** While the babies nurse, he can talk to them, shake rattles, or explain how his toys work. He can sing songs, make funny faces or show them his favorite stuffed animal.

- **Encourage bonding among all three.** Sometimes your older child just wants to sit and cuddle with you. He can snuggle up to his twin siblings as well and caress their arms and legs.

How to maintain your bond with your older child

Maybe you're worried not only about bonding with your twins, but maintaining the bond with your older child. You don't want him to feel like you love him any less, despite being busier with the twins.

It's important to always reiterate how much you love him, twins or not. Explain that being busy with the twins doesn't mean you love him any less, just like you still love him when you're away or cooking or at work.

Try a few of these activities to remind him just how much you love him:

- Include him in activities with the twins to help make him feel more involved in the process.

- Allow him to vent about the twins—don't shut down his emotions.

- The minute you have a chance (like once the twins are asleep), say, "Okay, let's hang out!" to show him you prioritize him over other tasks you could be doing in that time.

- Carve regular time to be with him, such as nightly story time or eating snacks together.

When the twins get all the attention

You'll come across others, from family to strangers, commenting on your twins. People will ask whether your babies are twins without mentioning your older child. Even family and friends might gush about the babies, sometimes to his confusion.

Based on your child's temperament, it's important to avoid alienating him from attention. Introverted children don't want attention, so it's easy to assume he's fine with it. Extroverted children might feel upset they're no longer the focus of conversations.

Sometimes it's not even a matter of him feeling left out, but rather confused at all the fuss about the twins. With all the twin talk going around, he might feel hyper-aware and anxious about what's to come or has already arrived.

What to do?

- **Let others know he's going to be a big brother.** Point out that your older child is going to be a big brother. They'll take the cue and congratulate him for his new role.

- **Ask him to show something he's proud of.** Maybe this is a new toy, a drawing he'd been working hard on, or that he can read a book all on his own. You're able to shift some of the attention to him as well.

- **Explain how much of a help he's been.** Has your little guy been extra attentive, or has he gone with you to a doctor's appointment? Let your friends and family know how much of a big help he's been with welcoming the twins.

- **Let him know people get excited about two babies.** Later in private, explain why people react so much with twins. How a new baby is a special occasion, and that having two babies doesn't happen often.

- **Ask friends and family to say hello to your older child first before meeting the twins.** Have them play with him as well as hold the babies.

- **Give him your attention.** When friends and family visit, use that as your opportunity to spend time with him. While they hold and fuss over the twins, you two can snuggle or read. After all, you're likely the favorite person whose attention he wants to get.

Now that you know how to handle your children, it's time to learn how to work as a team with your partner. The next chapter covers working together and supporting one another.

WORKING AS A TEAM
WITH YOUR PARTNER

Your relationship will go through ups and downs during your twin journey. It's crucial to keep communication open with your partner. Discuss both your expectations and desires as parents of twins. Don't assume he should just know or can read your hints.

You'll also want to discuss parenting topics now before the twins arrive. You'll continue to learn as you go along, but you can talk about how each of you imagine yourselves as parents.

Discussion topics to talk about:

- Will he attend doctor appointments during your pregnancy?
- Who will wake up for night feedings?
- How will you handle baby-related duties such as changing diapers and washing pump parts and bottles?
- How will you handle household chores such as preparing meals and taking out the trash?
- What are a few ways each of you can make life easier for the other?

Parenting practices to discuss:

- What sleeping habits do you want to establish with the twins?
- Do you prefer lots of visitors or not too many?
- What are your thoughts on breastfeeding and formula?

This discussion isn't set in stone as ammunition in potential future arguments. No "You told me you were okay with formula before!" I can't even tell you how many times I've changed my stance on many topics, but opening this discussion highlights many issues you may not know your partner feels. Talking about it now helps diffuse disagreements in the future.

Most importantly, you're establishing open communication. Don't keep it all in until you build resentment and explode at each other, or worse, take your frustration out on the kids.

Build a habit of talking openly, even about painful or awkward topics. Give each other the space and permission to speak without judging. Listen without thinking of a rebuttal or come up with your next thought when he hasn't even finished his sentence.

Here's another strategy to remind yourself you're on the same team: build a habit of talking to one another uninterrupted for at least 10 minutes each day. Carve out time when the TV's not on and the older kids have gone to bed and the twins are asleep (or at least quiet). Track whether you've had your "we time" every day.

It's easy to miss this uninterrupted time amid the chaos of twin life, but build open communication into your day so you can voice your concerns, laugh, or vent away your frustrations.

Find your common intentions

It's tempting to lash out at your partner because you're most comfortable with him. You know he'll accept you with all your imperfections. Still, remind yourself that it's not you vs him— it's you and him going through this crazy parenting journey.

You're on the same team. Take any argument you may have had: you'll see that beneath the differences, you both still have the same intentions—you just have different ways of getting there.

One of the best ways to remember this is to imagine how he's feeling. Yes, he snapped when he came home from work, something you didn't need after being home with the twins all day, but then you imagine how it feels like to plow through work sleep-deprived and drive that long commute. It doesn't excuse him, but you can also see how easy it is to snap.

Make a plan

Based on your discussions, draw a plan you can at least try. For instance, take nighttime wake-ups. Figure out a plan you can both agree on about how to handle who wakes up and what each of you do. Talking with several twin couples, a few examples include:

- Dad changes diapers and brings the twins to mom to nurse. Then they both burp one baby each.
- Dad changes diapers and both mom and dad take one baby each to bottle-feed and burp each baby.
- One parent takes the 9pm to 3am shift, and the other parent takes the 3am to 9am shift.
- Parents alternate evenings, so Dad wakes up Monday, Mom wakes up Tuesday, and so forth.
- Mom wakes up on weeknights and Dad wakes up on weekends.

And that's just for nighttime wake-ups! Draw a game plan using the above topics as a launching point.

With a plan and working as a team, you and your partner will tackle this twin business!

Best ways for your partner to support you

Even in these days, we think about child-rearing as a mom task, but I want to propose a mindset change: dads don't "help" moms. Your family and friends, yes, they help, but dads are equal co-parents to your twins, not babysitters or a helping hand. If you're in a position to have a partner in your life, you need to have him on board as an equal caregiver like yourself.

Because caring for twins is a challenge, many dads do this by default, but it's amazing how much we moms shoulder on ourselves as if we're doing this alone with help from our partners. Truly, the best way for dads to "help" is to assume an equal role in this journey.

So, what are a few ways dads can best support moms once the twins are born? How can he be an equal partner in parenthood?

Care for the twins to give mom a real break

Twin moms across the board said one of the best things dads can do is give us a real break!

Even if dad is with you all day, it's refreshing to step outside baby caring mode and be by yourself. Dad can care for the twins for several hours on a given day. This would allow you to enjoy hours and not just minutes of alone time.

Or maybe your break is shorter but more frequent. This could be something as simple as caring for the twins while you go for morning walks. Letting you sleep in on weekends or take regular naps.

Having your partner by your side is fantastic, but every so often, have him care for the twins alone so you can get a real break.

And just as important, do the same for him. Even if he's not with the twins as often, he still needs time for himself.

Hang out with your older children

You'll need to spend alone time with your older children, yes, but often, you'll juggle the needs of your twins with your older kids. Maybe you need to breastfeed, or you want to put them down for a nap without loud interruptions.

Dads can support moms by hanging out with your older children. He'll make sure he meets their needs so you can focus on the twins.

Wake up for nighttime feedings and changes

For many moms, especially those who breastfeed, nighttime wake-ups fall on their shoulders. After all, they're already waking up to nurse—why wake dad up as well?

Every family is different, and many will have arrangements between both parents on what works best for them, but with twins, it's crucial for dads to wake up or at least support moms during what is often the most difficult part of the day.

You're sleeping in hourly chunks, you're delirious, and you can't think straight. Morale may be at its lowest. Having dad wake up to do what he can makes nighttime much easier.

Even if you breastfeed, he can still wake up to bring you the twins. He can change diapers, fetch you anything you need, and burp one of the twins after. He can listen to your frustrations, and encourage you along.

Your routine may be different. Maybe you've decided that alternating evenings works best for both of you, or you divide late night and early morning shifts. Even if your partner doesn't wake up with you for every feeding, he can still take an active role in other ways.

Do helpful things around the house

With so much of your time devoted to the twins, a lot of household tasks will fall off your radar. For the most part, it's best to leave it at that. You don't need to maintain a spotless house during this newborn stage.

But some tasks can't be postponed too long, and here's where dads can pitch in. Taking out the trash while you're putting the twins to nap, for instance. Cooking breakfast and making sure your older child's lunch is packed for school. Filling up the car with gas before you head to an appointment.

Talk about your expectations and who does what. If need be, make a list of things you need to do and hang it on the fridge. Most important, have him pitch in as often as he can.

Encourage and motivate

Our partners can be some of the most positive cheerleaders we can have. When you feel discouraged, sad, or upset, turn to your partner to help you get through it. For instance, ask him to remind you of your breastfeeding goals, or talk about how you're coping with being a parent. Let him remind you of the positive things that outweigh the challenges.

And ask him to make you laugh! To remember the good times, watch a funny movie, bring you back to reality. These lighthearted moments can be all you need to keep going.

This chapter covered the many ways you and your partner can work together as a team. As you've seen, working together makes managing twins more doable. In the next chapter, I'll share practical ways for your friends and family to help with the twins.

BEST WAYS FOR
OTHERS TO HELP

If you have friends and family living nearby and willing to help, you're in luck. As they say, it takes a village to raise a child, and even more so when you have two. Friends and family can offer tons of help and support. Let's take a look at some of the best ways for them to do just that.

Bring food

Within the chaos of newborn twins, you, your partner, and your older kids still need to eat. With little time or inclination to cook, family and friends can fill that role by bringing food.

The food they bring doesn't always have to be ready-to-eat, either. Here a few ways to offer food when they visit:

- Simple ingredients to prepare a meal
- Home-cooked frozen meals
- Microwavable frozen meals
- Easy to cook meals like pasta and pasta sauce
- Household and grocery staples like milk, bread, and sugar
- Take-out from a restaurant
- And of course, ready-to-eat meals

Do household chores

As with cooking, cleaning will be low priority compared to caring for your twins, but you still need to maintain daily or weekly tasks, such as washing dishes and taking out the trash. Family and friends can help with these tasks as well.

A good trick? Hang a white board with dry-erase markers on a wall. List all the tasks you need to do around the house. When someone asks how they can help, direct them to the white board and they can take their pick. Even hanging it on the wall can be a subtle way for others to see how they can help without you outright asking for it.

A few common tasks include:

- Wash the dishes
- Empty and load dishes from the dishwasher
- Take out the trash and refill with new bags
- Wipe kitchen counters and other surfaces
- Wipe dining area surfaces
- Run the kids' laundry

Do errands

Your to-do list can extend beyond your home into errands outside. Your friends and family can help with running errands, especially if you're too tired to step outside.

Like your chores, write your errands on the white board or simply tell others when they ask how they can help. A few errands you might need help with include:

- Picking up food or ingredients at the grocery
- Driving you to an appointment
- Buying toiletries or medicine at the pharmacy
- Dropping off your mail
- Buying diapers and big items at the bulk store

Care for the twins

Most people who visit you will have one thing on their minds: to hold those precious babies! Even if it seems that's all your friends and family wants to do, let them. After all, you're with the twins all day and night. Handing them over to others can give you a much-needed break.

Explain a few of your ground rules, then allow them to fully care for your twins. Use this as an opportunity to take a long nap, a shower, or even run an errand. Spend time with your older child.

Friends and family are more rested than you are and don't mind holding the babies to sleep or comforting them through endless crying. Don't feel apologetic because caring for your twins is hard work. They know that. Let go of any guilt for handing baby duty to them for a little bit. This is as much of a treat for them as it is for you.

Spend time with your older child

Friends and family can also spend time with your older child. In fact, older kids would love the attention on them after the crazy changes that are happening.

Friends and family can play games, take your kids to the park, or prepare their snacks. Meanwhile, you can focus on your twins or nap while they sleep, all without worrying about your older child.

Stay for an extended time

Probably the best way for friends and family to help is to stay for an extended time. My mom spent the first three weeks at our home and was ready to lend a hand no matter the time of day or night.

This is especially useful because you'll have another adult who knows your routine just as you do. Rather than explaining your method to every new visitor, your extended guest knows exactly what to do. She knows which twin likes the pacifier and how to prepare oatmeal the way your child eats it. She'll be willing to stay up at nights knowing she'll go back to a full night's sleep in a few weeks.

It's for this reason many parents also hire a night nurse to help with nighttime duties. A night nurse can assume the tasks you'd normally have to do on your own.

Speaking of which, you can also...

Hire help

If you don't have a band of friends and family nearby to help, consider hiring help especially during the early weeks. Hiring a night nurse has helped tons of twin parents cope with the challenges of nighttime wake-ups.

You can also hire a cleaning service to handle household tasks and maintenance. Your neighbor's teenage daughter can be a mother's helper during the hours when you're alone with the twins, or you can look into other more traditional forms of childcare, even as early as the newborn stage. Nannies and au pairs would offer tremendous help with caring for two babies.

As you can see, caring for twins can often take a whole village. Even with my mom staying with us for a few weeks, I still felt like I could use a fourth adult. I joked we needed one adult per child, plus one more to take care of the house. It's hard work, and this is when you, your partner, family, and friends need to come together to make it as smooth as possible.

HOW TO ENCOURAGE INDIVIDUALITY IN TWINS

One concern parents have with raising twins is how to encourage their individuality. It's too easy for twins to feel lumped in together and identify with being a twin more so than being themselves. How can you celebrate their unique spirit that makes them who they are?

From infancy and onward, apply these tips to foster each twin's individuality.

Spend one-on-one time with each twin

Your twins will spend almost every minute with each other, not just staying at home or being out and about together. They'll likely do the same activities, from eating to sleeping to playing. It's just easier to "batch" their activities.

Switch things up by spending time with each twin. Snuggle with one toddler twin on the couch while the other is on the play mat. Take one out for an errand while another adult stays home with her twin.

Spending time alone with each parent is already recommended for children with siblings. With twins, it's even more important for them to bond with each parent.

Address them by their names, not only as "the twins"

Saying "the twins" is much easier, but if your kids grow up hearing them referred to as "the twins" all the time, they'll feel lumped in. This is especially more so if they have other siblings who aren't called "the twins."

Instead, refer to them by name, even if it takes longer to say "Chloe and Samantha." Doing so prioritizes their individuality more than their twin pairing.

Don't dress them alike all the time

Perhaps the easiest way to encourage individuality is to not dress them alike... at least not all the time. Coordinated outfits are fine, but so is having each child wear his own outfit. Besides, they'll go through a few onesies and outfits in a day, which makes matching them less doable.

Of course, it's cute to dress twins alike, and if you do, that's fine too! I do a bit of both, but tend to save coordinated outfits for special occasions.

Don't compare, especially with milestones and learning

With twins, you'll learn that each one develops on his own, regardless of his sibling. Try not to compare or worry if one twin isn't reaching milestones the other one already has.

After an older child and a set of twins, I can tell you they all develop differently. Kids reach milestones on their own timelines. Try not to compare or worry if one twin hasn't rolled over or walked yet.

Celebrate differences

Whether fraternal or identical, each child is unique. Celebrate their differences and what makes each one unique. Allow their personality to shine and their interests to blossom. You're not only welcoming a pair of twins, but two different and unique children!

SECTION 4:
PREPARING
FINANCIALLY

MANAGING THE COSTS OF
RAISING TWINS

Twins. Money. For many parents, the news of twins makes you wonder how you'll ever afford two babies at the same time. While you may have budgeted or expected for one baby, learning you have two comes as a huge shock.

My head was spinning thinking about all the costs of having twins. If you can relate, don't worry. This section covers how to prepare financially for twins. We'll talk about:

- One-time and recurring costs
- Financial strategies to implement now
- Effective ways to save money
- Overcoming the emotional side of money

The cost of twins is two-part. You have one-time costs to prepare for their arrival and recurring costs for after. I won't list expected costs for these since they vary so much from location to brand and even to your needs. Instead, I'll list the items themselves so you can gauge how much you should expect to spend.

Keep in mind these costs don't all happen at the same time. You won't need to buy high chairs until later, and your doctor co-pays will decrease once you give birth.

Preparing for one-time costs

As you prepare for your twins, you'll find yourself with a list of one-time costs. These are things you buy or spend money on just once or for a limited time and can include:

Hospital bills

Hospital bills can be one of the biggest expenses with caring for twins. You'll get the bill a few weeks or months after the twins are born.

Find out how much your insurance plan covers your hospital stay. You won't be able to predict the exact amount, but get a range of what to expect. You can begin saving now or at least setting aside the amount you need to pay it off.

Tip: If you have your own insurance apart from your spouse's, add yourself onto his too. You can use his as secondary insurance to cover anything your primary one doesn't. My primary insurance covered 90% of my hospital stay. Then my secondary insurance through my husband's employer covered the remaining 10%.

Baby gear

Added up, the baby gear you buy can affect your wallet. These are the items that will make up your registry and can include anything from cribs to nail clippers.

How to manage the expenses? I won't tell you to buy everything cheap. We all have different preferences. Instead, pick the absolute musts you don't want to scrimp on. Maybe you want the high-end organic crib mattress, or the jogging stroller because you want to exercise with your twins. Pick a few to splurge on, then budget everything else for lower expenses. Don't spend money on items you care little about and instead focus on the few that you do.

To cut down on costs even further, try these tips:

- **Don't pay full price.** Tons of baby stores offer coupons and price matching. Wait until a coupon or sale comes out, and plan your purchases then. A 20% off sale can be a huge saving if you're buying a $400+ double stroller.

- **Accept hand-me-downs or borrow from others.** Ask around or mention you're looking for certain items. Many parents want to part ways with baby gear, especially if it's taking up a ton of space in their home. I've received bassinets and bouncy seats and have given away baby monitors and bathtubs.

- **Make your registry list practical.** If you're making a public registry for friends and family, include items you couldn't borrow or get used. Let's say you're fine with getting a used rocking chair from a consignment store. Leave that out of your registry. Instead, ask for disposable items like diapers and wipes, or items you'd rather not buy used, such as baby bottles or car seats.

A car

With twins comes the need to fit two infant seats into your car. If you have older kids, you might have to reconsider your car arrangements. My husband and I both had sedans and were about to replace one of them when we found out about the twins. We were lucky we learned sooner rather than later because we were able to get a van instead of another sedan.

A few changes you might have to make include:

- Getting a different car that will fit all the car seats
- Keeping your current car and finding car seats that will fit (Diono has narrow car seats)
- Trading in your current car for a used or lower-cost one to reduce monthly payments
- Downsizing from two cars to one to eliminate monthly payments
- Finding alternative ways to commute (could one parent ride a bicycle to work or take the train?)

A house

Whew, take a deep breath! This might seem overwhelming, but some families do consider changing their housing situation because of the twins.

For me, we didn't have to move anywhere, even though we live in a two-bedroom apartment. The bedrooms are large, so we were able to fit two cribs as well as our eldest's twin bed.

Even if you're in a one-bedroom home, don't feel like you need to get into the housing market just yet. When I had my eldest, we were still in a one-bedroom unit and didn't move until he was 18-months-old. Not easy, for sure, having to share a bedroom with your baby and then toddler, but don't feel like you need to move right away to make space for your twins. Many twin parents put their twins to sleep in their bedroom anyway for the first several months.

That said, it's a good idea to think about your long-term housing plans for your family. Think about whether you want your twins to share a room or sleep in different ones, how much space they'll need once they outgrow toddler beds. While you don't have to rush into anything right now, you can begin to imagine or plan for years down the line.

Loss of income

Your loss of income is another money factor. You'll lose income during maternity leave or bed rest. Depending on your company or state, you might have less income coming in. If your partner takes paternity leave, he might lose income as well. And of course, your income will change if you decide not to return to work or work part-time.

Recurring costs to budget for

The other side of affording twins doesn't go away as easily: recurring costs. These range from large monthly expenses to smaller purchases that add up. Just as we did with one-time costs, we won't go into specific amounts. Our lifestyles and locations vary too much to place a dollar amount on these. Instead, I'll list expenses most twin parents will face.

- Childcare
- Diapers (or diaper service)
- Pump rental, parts, and storage bags
- Formula and bottles
- Solid food and supplies
- Clothing
- Toys and books
- Entertainment
- Laundry

- Toiletries
- Medicine
- Doctor visit co-pays
- Life insurance (for you)
- Health insurance
- College savings

Now that you know how much your costs will generally cost per month, let's dive into four financial strategies to prepare for your twins.

4 FINANCIAL STRATEGIES TO
PREPARE FOR TWINS

Thinking about your financial future raising twins is daunting. You might have mild panic attacks wondering how you'll ever make it work. You're already missing your disposable income, both for leisure and savings.

We all have different financial backgrounds. We have different incomes and live in different parts of the world. We may or may not have the financial support or safety net of family.

But one thing we have in common is the new reality of raising twins and the costs that go along with it. I'll cover four strategies you can implement to start you off on the right foot.

1. Start saving now

Saving money before your twins have arrived has so many benefits. Setting aside money gives you a buffer for leaner times. You'll have a cushion during maternity leave or cash for childcare. Set aside as much as you're comfortable with so you can dip into that account should you need to.

Let's say you're earning a full-time income now but you're not sure you can afford a nanny for a set number of years. Put your extra savings into your bank account now while you have disposable income. You can use it down the line to cover the rest of your childcare costs.

Another tactic with saving money is to live like your future self. If you expect living off of a percentage of your salary, budget that amount into your finances now. Pretend you're already paying for childcare or buying baby gear or living on less income. When the twins arrive, you're already used to it and won't feel shocked. Better yet, you'll have money set aside in case you need to use it.

2. Budget for recurring costs

Earlier, we talked about recurring costs you can expect every month. List the costs you can expect to have. Thinking of the big picture helps you see where your options are. If your income isn't going to cover your monthly expenses, see which areas of your budget you can trim. Some of these are minor like buying used baby items. Others need bigger actions like selling a car.

With a big picture image of your new lifestyle, you're able to face your reality with brutal honesty. Make the changes necessary now before the twins arrive. You may even be able to use the money you saved from the first strategy (save money now) to cover extra monthly costs.

3. Earn extra income

Most financial advice tells you to save money to prepare for your twins. Saving is one of the easiest ways to cut down costs and afford two babies, but on the other side of saving money is something most people don't consider: earning more money.

You may not think you're at the stage where you can earn extra income, but stay with me. One key reason you shouldn't ignore the earning side of money is because you have no cap on how much you can earn. You can only save and penny pinch to a limit. After a while, you won't be able to save if you have nothing left to save.

But earning income has no limits. You can earn as much as you're willing to be creative or spend time on your efforts. Let's take a look at a few ways you can earn extra income to help prepare you for life with twins:

- **Sell old items.** You're bound to find something you hardly use and may sell well. Look up sites like eBay or Craigslist to sell your old stuff, or hold an old-fashioned garage sale.

- **Make and sell items.** You might have made jewelry in the past that you can sell on Etsy, or digital files and products like printables or spreadsheets. There are so many ways to make money from something you may already be doing.

- **Freelance.** Can you offer a service on the side, maybe even related to your profession? Think about offering services, from calligraphy to graphic design to baking cakes.

- **Perform well at work to deserve a raise.** Asking for a raise because you're having twins is never a good idea, but you can think of ways to up your game to deserve one. Discuss your goals and performance with your employer and talk about your expectations.

- **Rent your property.** Extra income can also include renting property, such as a spare or detached room in your home. If you're comfortable with the process, renting property gives you steady income every month.

Most of your long-term efforts will likely fall into the savings category. Still, I encourage you to look into ways you can also earn money. Some of them might be one-time events like holding a garage sale. Others can have a long-lasting impact like getting a raise.

Part of feeling stressed about twins and money is because there's only so much you can save, but with earning more income, you'll find different ways to manage the financial crunch.

4. Stay healthy

We all know we should stay as healthy as possible when we're pregnant, but if you need more motivation, consider how many costs you avoid with a healthy lifestyle! You can't predict medical complications, even if you were as diligent as possible, but the more you take care of yourself, the more likely you'll have less to worry about.

These are some of the challenges you avoid by staying as healthy as possible:

- Extra doctor co-pays and prescriptions for complications
- Taking sick or unpaid days
- Earlier bed rest (and less full-time income)
- Premature delivery and NICU hospital stays and bills

I know how hard it is to be healthy during a difficult twin pregnancy. You can't bother with eating vegetables or lean proteins when you'd rather throw up. Walking around the block gets more tiresome by the week, and you can't seem to avoid the stress at work.

But focus on a healthy pregnancy when possible. Choose healthy meals at restaurants and follow your doctor's recommendations. Get the rest your body needs. Staying healthy can make a huge impact on your financial picture.

One of the easiest ways to cut costs is to look at where you can save money the most. In the next chapter, we'll learn all the ways you can save for your twins.

EFFECTIVE WAYS TO
SAVE MONEY

If you're like most twin moms, you're looking for ways to save money before and after your twins arrive. These are the different ways I and other twin moms I spoke with have saved big bucks, even with caring for two.

Before the twins arrive

- **Don't buy two of everything.** You might assume you need two of everything, but often you're fine with just one. Sometimes you're not sure whether you need two. In that case, either buy both but don't open it in case you need to return it, or buy just one and see if you really need two of them.

- **Buy low- to mid-price gear.** Spend money on items you value. Be picky with what you spend money on, whether that's cribs or diapers. Then don't spend a lot on the others.

- **Stick to certain brands you know aren't as expensive as others.** Buy generic or store brands instead of other more popular ones.

- **Use a flexible spending account.** See if your work offers a flexible spending account. You can set aside a portion of your salary toward medical-related expenses such as hospital bills or prescriptions. The money is taken out before taxes, so you're saving the same amount of your current tax bracket.

- **Accept hand-me-downs.** Spread the word you're expecting and you'll find yourself receiving baby items from others. People can't wait to get rid of their stuff. Don't turn anything down just yet!

- **Shop at consignment stores.** Consignment stores are like thrift stores for baby clothes and gear. You'll find a ton of good stuff in these stores. I've also sold items here and know first hand how picky they are with what they accept. Look for things your twins need but know they'll outgrow quickly, like cold weather outerwear, and it's perfect for big-ticket items you'd love to have without spending a lot of money on.

- **Always use a coupon.** If you decide to buy new, you can still snatch good deals by using coupons. Babies R Us often offers coupons for one-time purchases. They also hold sales for certain gear, like a stroller sale. Short story: Don't pay full price. Other stores like Buy Buy Baby even offer price matches. Look out for sales and coupons to get even better deals.

- **Ask for samples and coupons.** Many companies are willing to send samples or high-value coupons to twin moms. You can send an email with photos of your twins' crib cards explaining you're a new twin mom who'd love to try their products. This is a great way to get samples and coupons for ongoing expenses like formula and diapers.

- **Make big changes.** You can also take savings to the extreme and make big changes in your life. Use this strategy if your savings strategies aren't sustainable. Downsize your home or car or get rid of monthly payments for cable or your cell phone. Think about your major expenses and get creative with how you can slash that by a lot.

- **Adopt a frugal lifestyle.** Living frugally before and after your twins arrive is one of the smartest things you can do. Frugal living isn't about deprivation. Instead, think of it as being really picky with what deserves your hard-earned money. Spend on what matters, then save on the rest.

  Cook from scratch most days, then splurge on a restaurant meal once in a while. Ask yourself if you really need something before buying it. Then only buy the items you especially want or need, and find creative ways to get the same things but cheaper or for free. Borrow DVDs for free at the library instead of watching them in the theater.

After the twins arrive

- **Change your work schedule.** Save money after the twins arrive by changing your work schedule or arrangement. See if you or your partner can work a flexible schedule to lessen childcare hours, or ask Grandma to care for them a few days a week to reduce childcare costs. It'll also give her an opportunity to spend time with the twins.

- **Hire a nanny.** In many areas, hiring a nanny to care for your twins is less expensive than placing them in day care. Even with sibling discounts, you might be better off hiring a nanny and negotiating a rate. Extra perks include not having to pack and load two babies or disrupting their schedule.

- **Shop in bulk stores or Amazon Family.** With Amazon Family, you can order baby items and diapers with deep discounts.

I bought most of my baby items through Costco, such as diapers, wipes, formula, and body wash.

- **Breastfeed.** Breastfeeding saves you money from not having to buy formula. The only associated costs with breastfeeding is a pump or pump rental, accessories and extra food. Even the pump and accessories are optional if you decide to nurse exclusively.

- **Make your own baby food.** Once your twins are ready for solids, make your own baby food to cut down on costs. Initial investments include a blender (which you might already have) and food storage containers. They're also usually better tasting and more nutritious than their jarred counterparts.

- **Ask for twin discounts.** You'll be surprised how many stores and businesses offer discounts for twins. Babies R Us and Buy Buy Baby offer discounts if you buy two of the same item.

- **Stock up on sales.** Many stores like Target, Costco, or Babies R Us hold sales on certain items. When they do, stock up to cover yourself for the next few weeks or months.

Look for creative ways to save money, both before and after the twins arrive. Make saving and earning extra income a lifestyle change so you don't feel swamped in the years down the line.

So far, we've covered tactics and strategies to financially plan for your twins, but what if money is more of an emotional subject for you? In the next chapter, we'll talk about managing the emotional side of money.

MANAGING THE
EMOTIONS OF MONEY

You've read strategies on saving and earning money. You've also learned about how to budget for your twins. Now we'll go into the less tangible side of finances and talk about the emotions about money.

For many moms, grappling with the emotional side of money is one of the toughest challenges. We feel vulnerable or unsure how it'll all work out. It's overwhelming to think about everything you'd need to spend money on, and we wonder if we'd be able to provide as well as we thought we could.

How to cope with your fears and worries about money

The good news? Our fears and worries are emotions based on past assumptions and future projections. We assume things will get crazy because of what we've experienced in the past, and we project worst-case scenarios even though we don't have anything solid to back it up.

Our worries and fears can get pretty intense at first, but by listing out and following these four steps, you can manage your emotions and be more proactive:

1. What are you worried about?

2. What is the absolute worst-case scenario you can imagine? Add to that: What is a terrible outcome you're imagining?

3. What can you do right now to avoid either scenarios?

4. Down the line, record what ended up happening.

Be proactive with your worries and fears. They serve a purpose, if only to remind us what we still need to do, but don't allow them to consume you into inaction. Look into resources and options for what you can do, even writing them down on your calendar and to-do list. These steps will ease your worries and guide you towards positive action.

Avoid comparisons and guilt traps

I was skimming through a Facebook mommy group when I saw this post:

"$300 for satin crib sheets. Retails for $800!"

The mom also included photos of their impeccable nursery, complete with chandeliers. My mood melted, and I knew why: I was comparing myself to other people. It's easy to base your worth and self-esteem on your surroundings.

No matter our lifestyles, we're all prone to compare or feel guilty about how we provide. We see our friends who own beautiful homes. Relatives who travel all over the world. Moms who stay home with their kids while we feel guilty for working. Meanwhile, we're poring through coupons or wondering how we'll ever afford day care.

It seems unfair.

It's so easy to feel jealous of what others have and what we don't. On top of all that, we feel inadequate or guilty for not being able to give our kids all we want to provide.

What can you do when you start comparing yourself to others?

Be grateful

Gratitude highlights how much we already have, rather than focusing on what we don't. It reminds us that we have enough, even when it seems that others keep wanting more. And it reminds us of the many things to be thankful for—things that others would be just as envious of.

You wonder why you're living in an apartment when everyone else has a backyard. So feeling grateful for having a spacious apartment can do wonders.

Or you assume life would be better if you had more money, but you remember to be grateful that you even have an income.

Think about all the good things you have, and you'll see how other people wish they were in your position.

Set goals

Rather than allowing comparisons to bring you down, set goals instead. Turn the comparisons into goals you'd like to achieve.

If you're jealous of your friend who's home with her kids, look for ways to make that possible for yourself.

If someone else seems to have exactly what you wish you had, study their methods. What are they doing to get to where they are? What can you learn from them, and how can you apply it to your own life?

Do what you can to make the changes you want to happen. Squirrel money away into a vacation fund. It may take longer, but you'll still be able to take one rather than feeling like you can't afford to go anywhere. Some comparisons aren't all bad: use them to motivate you to improve your life.

Delete

Remember that mommy post with the $300 satin crib sheets? After a few more of those posts, I decided to hide that Facebook group for a while. I didn't want to check Facebook only to find yet another post or complaint I couldn't relate to.

Unplug from technology or the Internet. Less television, news, or digital media means you have less lives to hold yourself up against. Sometimes we need to get rid of comparisons by removing the sources to begin with.

When your partner is the one freaking out

If your partner is like many twin dads, he may have had a slight freak-out moment when he found out about twins. He likely wondered whether he's fit to be a dad. Whether he'd know what to do in crisis moments, and, of course, whether he can provide for his double bundles.

Many men see their role in the family as the provider, even if both parents work, and even if the woman earns more money. For many dads, news of twins challenges their roles and makes them feel vulnerable. Like they have less control.

So your partner might immerse himself in spreadsheets and budgets. He might cramp down on your budget, even if you have lots of wiggle room. He might get apprehensive about every baby purchase you make.

He might not admit to feeling nervous or scared, but this may be his way of coping with the unknown. He feels a loss of control and is over-compensating by doing all he can do to prepare for the twins. He might be thinking into the future, things like college savings or extracurricular activities, so much so that he is doing everything he can now to prepare or avoid potential problems.

If he's driving you crazy, talk to him about his fears and worries. Encourage him to take it day by day, and to plan for the next year and no more than that. It's hard to imagine every scenario possible, especially so far down the line. Make sure you're covered for the next year, then adjust your strategy as you go along. You may find you need to be tighter with money, or that you actually had a lot more wiggle room than you budgeted for.

SECTION 5:
WHAT TO BUY

TWIN BABY REGISTRY
MUST-HAVES

With twins on the way, the baby gear you need will be different from a typical singleton pregnancy. Except what exactly do you need? And do you need two of everything? This lesson will dive into the twin baby gear you need, plus exactly how many of each you'll need to get, starting with items for sleeping.

Sleeping

2 cribs: I suggest buying cribs that can convert to toddler beds, so you won't have to buy a separate toddler bed after the crib. You'll just go from crib/toddler bed to twin bed instead of crib to toddler bed to twin bed. Tip: You may not need your cribs right away. It's good to have them set up, but you can also put your twins to sleep in bassinets. They usually prefer small quarters.

2 mattresses: Each crib will need its own mattresses. I splurged on mattresses and went with an organic brand. Whichever you decide, I recommend you get a waterproof mattress. Your babies will leak at some point, and waterproof mattresses help with clean-up.

6 fitted crib sheets: You'll want extra sheets around when your twins soil themselves in the cribs. I loved those from Organic Cotton. I'm more of a no-pattern kind of girl, and their cream fitted sheets were versatile, soft, and organic.

2 bassinets: Babies love to sleep in confined spaces—it reminds them of their time in the womb. Bassinets are a fantastic option if your twins don't take to cribs. I didn't think my twins needed a bassinet and so didn't get them before they arrived. Eventually I learned how much better they slept in smaller spaces. I ended up buying one and borrowing another from a friend. Well worth it!

4 Velcro swaddles or sleep suits: Ready-to-go swaddles and suits don't come undone as often as your standard baby blanket. A must for middle-of-the-night wake-ups when you're too sleepy to do the full swaddle routine. Swaddles keep your twins snug and help them sleep longer.

4 thick blankets: Use these to cover your babies in the car seat or to lay them on the floor for tummy time (or even nap time).

4 light blankets: Light blankets like Aden+Anais blankets work great for light and loose swaddles. Use them for burp cloths, breastfeeding covers, or blankets to keep the sun out of your babies' eyes when they're in the stroller.

4 pacifiers: Your twins might take to sucking on pacifiers to soothe and even help them fall asleep.

4 sleep sacks: If your twins don't sleep with a swaddle (or they've outgrown them), another great option is sleep sacks. Regular blankets aren't safe for babies to sleep with in the crib. Sleep sacks keep them warm without the risks of a regular blanket.

1 white noise machine (or 2 if they're in separate rooms): White noise machines help twins sleep longer because they drown out the sounds that might startle them awake. This could be anything from noise outside the house to you walking around and even each other's cries. Marpac and HoMedics are a few to check out. An alternative to a white noise machine is a regular fan or heater, or even downloaded music or apps on your iPhone.

1 baby monitor: If you want to check on your twins without opening the door, a baby monitor is the way to go. This is especially useful if your room is far from theirs—you can set the monitor next to your bedside table.

Breastfeeding

1 twin nursing pillow: A twin nursing pillow will allow you to tandem feed, or feed both twins at the same time. This step alone can save you so much time! I used the My Brest Friend twin pillow, and other moms have also used the Twin Z pillow.

1 extra nursing pillow cover: In addition to the cover that comes with your pillow, get another one in case your twins soil it.

16-20 burp cloths: Don't get your typical small burp cloths. Instead, get the ones that look like cloth diapers. Start with 16-20, and get more if one or both your twins spit up often.

Lanolin cream: Applying lanolin cream to your nipples before and after nursing can help prevent and heal soreness.

Nursing cover: I simply used the sheer Aden+Anais swaddle blankets, but you can also get a cover specifically for nursing.

Bottle-feeding

Formula: Get one six-pack of ready-to-use formula and one container of powdered. Formula is one of those things you might have to experiment with in case your twins don't take to a particular brand or kind of formula. I'd hate for you to get formula in bulk and realize afterward that your twins don't take to them. I used Enfamil for my twins with no issues.

12 bottles: After much trial and error, I settled on Playtex Vent-Aire bottles. I like how there aren't a million parts to clean but they're still designed to reduce gas in the babies.

1 bottle brush: The Oxo brush stands up in a sturdy base so you don't keep knocking it over like other brands.

1 (large) drying rack: I love Boon drying racks, and now they come in a large size. They're versatile and can fit anything from bottle parts to utensils and bowls.

Pumping

1 double electric pump: Try to get or rent a hospital-grade pump like the Medela Symphony. These are more efficient and hardier than a regular pump. However, a standard electric pump will work if you don't plan to pump regularly. No matter what, get a double pump, not single, to cut your pumping time by half.

2 sets of pump parts: Two sets of pump parts ensure you're always ready to pump even if your current parts are broken or unwashed. If you get a Medela pump, get several of the white membranes and bring those with you (or leave them at work). They're fragile and can tear easily.

1 hands-free pump bra: This is one of those purchases where I thought, How did I ever last without it? It's such a game changer with pumping since you can free up your hands. Simple Wishes makes a fantastic hands-free pump bra.

1 insulated bottle tote: Keep your pumped milk fresh with an insulated bottle tote. Use this for pumping and for being out and about with your twins.

1 box of breast milk storage bags: These are much easier to bring to work than bottles. They're also a must if you plan to freeze and store breast milk.

Eating solids

You won't need the items below until your twins are about 4-6 months old and eating solids:

2 high chairs: Each baby will need his or her own high chair to eat. A few recommended products include Ikea Antelop, Ingenuity, Graco Blossom 4-in-1 and Inglesina Gusto. You can also attach a portable "booster seat" if you want to use a current dining room chair as a high chair.

16 bibs: Like burp cloths, you may have more or less depending on how often you wash. Bibs are good to have on hand not just for feeding, but for wiping drool all day.

4 sets of baby food storage containers: I love the Oxo food containers. They stack for easy storage. They're designed to freeze as well as store in the fridge, and they reheat easily.

4 plates and utensils: I love Oxo plates because they have a removable ring (for easier scooping) and a rubber base. It can also come with a fork and spoon set.

6 sets of bowls: Use bowls for regular meals as well as for taking snacks with you on the go. Get sets with large and small sizes.

Bathing

1 infant bathtub: Bathing is usually a one-at-a-time task, so you don't need two bathtubs. Get an infant bathtub with a mesh top that looks like a hammock. This will be essential for keeping them from being submerged in water (because you can't wet their umbilical cords until they fall off). Once their umbilical cords have fallen off, you simply remove the mesh top.

14-20 washcloths: Depending on how often you wash laundry and bathe your twins, you'll need anywhere from 14-20 washcloths. Use these, along with a baby body wash, to gently wipe their bodies. Pay special attention to little cracks and folds you may forget, such as underarms or under the knees.

1 shampoo/body wash: I'm a big fan of Johnson's body wash. After trying other brands, this was the only one that wouldn't sting my babies' eyes.

Bath toys: Once your twins can sit up, keep bath time fun for your twins with simple bath toys. Some of my favorites include toys that squirt, foam alphabet letters, and waterproof books.

4 towels: Hooded towels cover your twins' heads and keep the surface you lay them on dry. Regular baby towels also work but sometimes our bed would get wet from their heads when we'd lay them down.

1 toddler bathtub: As with the infant bathtub, you'll only need one of these. Eventually your babies will outgrow the infant bathtub and will need a larger toddler bathtub. Something big enough for them to fit but small enough that they're not overwhelmed sitting in an empty bathtub. Keep in mind that you can get this much later, when they're about 9-10 months old and can sit comfortably on their own.

1 bathtub faucet cover: Again more down the line, a faucet cover is a good option to have once they're bathing in an actual bathtub and might slip and slide.

Diaper changes

1 changing table with drawers to put clothes in: I'm a fan of changing tables that also serve as a place to store clothes. Even better if they have shelves for cubbies to hold diapers, wipes, and other essentials. You might get away with changing on the floor or your bed, but it's more convenient and easier on your back to change the twins with a changing table.

1 changing pad: With a changing table, you'll need one changing pad. These usually come as waterproof pads with a safety belt to buckle your twins.

3 changing pad covers: You'll also need about 3 changing pad covers. These are like "fitted sheets" that go over the changing pad.

1 diaper pail: I suggest getting a diaper pail with odor control if you don't plan to change the pail frequently. For breastfed babies, you might get away with using a regular trash can, since their poop won't smell. (At least until they begin eating solids a few months later.)

2 boxes of newborn diapers: Your twins will likely go through at least 2 standard diaper boxes a month. Since most twins are born on the small size, it's safe to say you'll want to get the newborn size instead of size 1.

1 tub of diaper cream: Triple Paste is the way to go. Keep a tub of diaper cream in your changing table to prevent and heal diaper rash. You might also want to keep a smaller tube in your diaper bag.

For the home

2 bouncer seats: These seats work great for many functions. They entertain your twins since many come with toys and lights they can play with. You can also use them for bottle feeding at the same time once your twins can sit upright well. And they're portable—you can keep your babies nearby and take them with you around the house.

1 swing: I sometimes wished I had 2 swings, but even 1 will do wonders. Swings will help your twins fall asleep, especially if they need motion.

On the go

2 baby carriers or wraps: Baby carriers and wraps allow you to strap your twins close to you. Wraps in particular keep them snug and are a great way for your twins to fall asleep in a comfortable position. They're also convenient for going out and about if you plan to walk with another adult (one twin each) and avoid using the stroller.

1 double stroller: Double strollers come in two options: side-by-side or tandem. Recommended brands include City Select, Baby Trend Sit and Stand, Mountain Buggy Duet, and the Chicco Keyfit 30. You'll use your double stroller for everything (even getting them out of your car), so pick wisely!

A few parents have asked what to do if you have an older child—do you get a double or triple stroller? It's usually better to get a double stroller and either:

- Have your older child walk,
- Wear one twin in a carrier or wrap and place the other in the double stroller with your older child, or
- Purchase a standing board you can attach to the stroller that your older child can stand on.

1 diaper bag: You don't need two diaper bags for your twins. Instead, get one that's roomy and functional. SkipHop makes a great diaper bag for multiples, as does Baby Bjorn. You'll want a diaper bag with compartments to separate diapers and wipes from food and pacifiers. Extra points if your diaper bag has insulation for bottles.

Clothing

Start with these in newborn sizes.

- 14 onesies
- 8 long-sleeve onesies
- 10 footed zip pajamas
- 14 pairs of socks
- 6 pairs of pants
- 6 pairs of shorts

Toiletries

- 1 pair of nail clippers
- 1 nose sucker
- Vitamin D drops for breastfed babies

- 1 comb
- 1 thermometer

This is a lot to take in, so don't feel overwhelmed with all your options. At the end of the day, your twins will be fine whether they have one kind of stroller instead of the other.

Not sure if you should get something or not? Buy as you go. Decide down the line whether you truly need an item or not. Some twin moms can get by with one swing while others swear by two. While others needed gas drops from the start, you might find you don't need them at all, or at least until much later.

Don't feel pressured to buy everything just now. Save your baby shower gift cards for after the twins' arrival when, in the trenches of it all, you can better decide what you truly need.

With your must-have list, now you know exactly what to get right away, how many you'll need for twins, and the items you can buy later.

HOW TO BUY MATERNITY CLOTHES

Buying maternity clothes for a twin pregnancy isn't the same as carrying a singleton. Maternity clothes aren't typically created for moms of multiples, so you'll need to be smart and creative about stocking up on maternity clothes. Keep these pointers in mind as you build your wardrobe:

Buy as you need

With maternity clothes, you don't want to buy everything all at once, and not in the beginning stages of pregnancy. Whereas you can stock up on baby gear, keep maternity clothes on a buy-as-you-need basis. Your body will grow depending on many factors, like whether this is your first pregnancy or how much weight you gain.

Your best bet is to buy maternity clothes as you outgrow your current wardrobe. Maybe that's when you can't fit into even your regular yoga pants, or when you need to upgrade to a larger maternity size because you're carrying twins.

Use what you can from your current wardrobe

You'll be surprised how far you can stretch some of your current clothes. Some styles lend themselves to pregnancy. Depending on your body type, you may be able to wear things like your yoga pants, maxi dresses, or cardigans through at least some of your pregnancy.

Look for clothes with room to give

You might see a few tight-fitting pieces of maternity clothes designed for pregnancy. Word of warning: this won't last you all the way through your final weeks. From things like tops that hug to even sweater tops, many maternity clothes are designed for singleton pregnancies.

Instead, choose loose-fitting maternity clothes with room to give. These will last much longer than tighter-fitting ones.

Buy sizes above your pre-pregnancy size

Most maternity clothing brands base sizes on your pre-pregnancy sizes. So if you were a medium before pregnancy, you'd typically want to buy medium maternity clothes.

Except you're carrying multiples, which isn't typical. During the second trimester, you can get away with buying your pre-pregnancy size, but as you near the final weeks, be prepared to buy a few sizes above your pre-pregnancy size.

Remember when I said to buy as you go? This is when it becomes even more important to buy maternity clothes as you need them. There's no telling which brands or sizes will fit you in the future. Instead, as you feel yourself outgrowing maternity clothes, keep buying a few sizes up.

Stick to basic patterns and styles

It's common to only buy a few pieces of maternity clothes and wear them over and over. You won't have the type of wardrobe where you'll wear a top once or twice because you have so many. Instead, you'll settle on a few good pieces and rotate, mix, and match.

That's why you should try to stick to basic patterns and styles. Stick to solid colors so you feel like you can wear them frequently without seeming like you are. Choose regular cuts and styles instead of strange or trendy, and pick colors that match well with others such as neutrals over bright colors.

Your maternity clothes must-haves

Now that you know what to look for, what exactly should you get? As with anything clothes, this is all preference. Still, there are a few pieces you should consider as your must-haves:

- Yoga pants
- Leggings
- Maternity jeans
- Maxi or loose dresses
- Tank tops or nursing tops
- Larger bras
- Sweater or outerwear if it's cold
- Several tops for work or outside
- Sleepwear

SECTION 6:
BALANCING TWINS AND WORK

GETTING THROUGH WORK
AND YOUR TWIN
PREGNANCY

A common struggle for twin moms is balancing your new life with work. Maybe you're new in your pregnancy and nauseous every day, or you're nearing the end of it and have no idea how much longer you can keep working. You may be wondering how you'll manage going back to work once the twins arrive.

In this section, we'll talk all about work and how to get through some of the most challenging days. You'll learn how to:

- Get through work and your twin pregnancy
- Decide when to stop working
- Perform well at work before and after the twins arrive
- Transition back to work after maternity leave

Getting through work and your twin pregnancy

Getting through work while pregnant with twins is a huge challenge for many moms. You might need to travel for work, or stay on your feet for hours, or attend back-to-back meetings. All while trying to stay engaged and focused on your tasks.

What might seem tolerable in a regular pregnancy feels worse with twins. Many of our symptoms surface much sooner.

Combine those challenges with needing to perform at work, and it can be difficult to juggle the two.

In this chapter, you'll learn how to maximize your time at work while taking care of your pregnancy needs.

Keep your morning sickness remedies nearby

Morning sickness is worse when you're not in the comfort or privacy of your home. You're expected to function and look normal all while feeling extra tired and nauseous.

Keeping your go-to remedies nearby offers a much-needed relief to an otherwise long day. A few things to keep handy are:

- Ginger tea
- Lemon drops
- Mints and gum
- A water bottle
- Healthy snacks

If you can't stomach a real meal, nibble on healthy snacks throughout the day. You'll more likely keep food in your stomach when you snack in bits and pieces. Plus, the constant food keeps your blood sugar steady (and nausea at bay).

Take much-needed breaks

The downside of working in a typical workplace is the lack of breaks a pregnant twin mom needs. We're supposed to rest as much as possible, but expected to work eight hours.

Instead, take frequent breaks. You might want to:

- Step outside for fresh air
- Nap if possible
- Take deep breaths at your desk
- Stand up periodically so you're not sitting all day (and vice versa: sit down as much as you can if you're on your feet)
- Go for a walk if your body can still handle it
- Chat with a co-worker

Sometimes, even resting your head in your hands for a few minutes at your desk is necessary. It can be tough plugging through the day, so even the tiniest of breaks can add up.

Make yourself comfortable

Along with taking frequent breaks, make yourself comfortable at work. Balance your workplace dress code with a comfortable but appropriate wardrobe. Once your belly gets bigger, you'll want to stick to flats instead of high heels. If the weather allows it, sandals are a great option. They're flat, roomy, and wide enough to accommodate possible feet swelling.

Even though you're dressing for your profession, being pregnant means you can "dress down." No need to buy a whole new maternity wardrobe when more casual clothes will do.

You also might want to place a box or a footstool under your desk to elevate your feet. They can get swollen, so raising them above ground can relieve that pressure.

And if you're nervous about needing a quick exit from meetings to run to the bathroom, sit near the door. You can leave more discreetly if you're feeling nauseous, need to use the restroom, or get some fresh air.

Getting through work while pregnant with twins is tough. Maybe you've even wondered when you should leave work. In the next chapter, we'll talk about when to leave work as well as other ways to cut back on work.

DECIDING WHEN TO
STOP WORKING

Ask twin moms when they stopped working and you'll get a whole slew of answers from both ends. Some worked all the way up to 38 weeks while others stopped the minute they got pregnant. Each mom's decision of when to keep working and when to stop depends on several factors.

Regardless of the reasons, twin moms tend to leave work much sooner than singleton moms. With my singleton, my last day coincided with the day I got contractions, so I worked all the way up through labor. With my twins, I was on bed rest at 31 weeks and I didn't get contractions until closer to 36 weeks.

A twin pregnancy has complications that make it difficult to work as long as a regular pregnancy. It's not so much "planning" when to leave work as it is listening to your body and considering these factors:

Factors to consider when deciding when to stop

Your job

Certain jobs take a more physical and mental toll on a twin pregnancy. Think about how much time you spend standing on your feet or working longer than an eight-hour day. Some jobs aren't conducive to pregnancy, like being around chemicals or lifting heavy items.

Other times, it's the mental strain of a job that does you in. A toxic work environment and its stresses make it harder to keep working. A long commute can take a toll on your energy. Consider how your job either drains or fills your bucket.

The kind of twins you're having

Your doctor might advise you to leave work earlier than even other twin moms because of the kind of twin pregnancy you have. Moms with Mo/Mo twins are at the highest risk and tend to leave work early to avoid complications.

Your complications

Meanwhile, twin moms without complications are the ones most likely to work all the way up to labor. Certain complications also simply call for you to stop working and go on bed rest or even deliver your twins. For instance, pre-eclampsia symptoms might mean strict monitoring at the hospital.

Your finances

Unfortunately, finances still play a big role on when to leave work. Differences in state and workplace policies mean not all moms have the same maternity leave coverage. Some companies and states offer paid leave, while others leave you relying on savings or accrued vacation time.

Try to save both money and vacation hours while you're still working. Start a "baby fund" you can dip into should you suddenly need to leave work earlier than anticipated so you won't feel pinched. Vacation hours you save now can go towards either before or after the baby is born.

Alternatives to leaving work

Let's say you want to keep working as long as possible but not with your current schedule. Discuss with your employer several options that can work for both of you. You can:

- **Reduce your hours.** Working part-time can give you the income you need without putting your body and mind through the gruel of a full-time schedule. Even leaving an hour early each day can make all the difference.

- **Work from home a few days.** Keep your full-time income but ask if you can work from home a few days of the week. This can save you time on the road and allow you to work in the comfort of your home.

- **Work from home completely.** Modified bed rest, which I went on at 30 weeks, can include working from home completely. Your doctor might have you working on a laptop lying down, or you could be allowed to work sitting upright.

What happens, though, if you have no complications but want to stop working because you just can't take it anymore?

Talk to your doctor about leaving early. Many doctors prefer twin moms to stop working around 28 to 32 weeks (though of course this varies with each case). You don't need a medical complication to stop working other than feeling like your health will fare better without going to work.

Like I mentioned in the beginning, listen to your body. If it's telling you to take it easy and you can manage financially, you're better off taking care of yourself now before complications do arise.

If it's financial costs you're concerned about, remember that premature babies and the NICU cost more than the time off you took from work. Financial reasons aside, the longer you can keep the twins in your belly, the better.

Real twin mom stories

Take a look at some working twin moms' stories of when they decided to (or had to) stop working:

- "I'm a kindergarten teacher. I stopped at 30 weeks and I wasn't on bed rest—it just got hard to keep up."

- "My plan was to work up until the Friday before my scheduled C-section. It didn't work out like that—I worked until the day they came at 37 weeks."

- "I worked from home full-time up until the minute I went into labor. I continued working part-time from the hospital for 3-4 weeks while my twins were in the NICU."

- "I stopped working at 29 weeks. I went into preterm labor and got it stopped. I tried to go back to work, but contractions wouldn't stop until I just rested my mind and body. Even working from home was too much. I made it to 34 weeks."

- "My doctor asked me to stop work at 26 weeks. Not bed rest, but she just wanted me off my feet. I had my scheduled

C-section at 37 weeks."

- "My OB suggested that I have everything wrapped up by 32 weeks, so I started working from home at 32.5 weeks. My DiDi twins came at 34.5 weeks (two weeks before my scheduled C-section)."

- "I stopped working at 26 weeks. I'm a hospital nurse, and at 20 weeks I started working at a desk job. It was flexible hours and they told me to just keep coming for as long as I could. By 26 weeks, I got too tired and didn't want to risk going early. I made it to 36.3 weeks."

- "I was scheduled to be induced at 37 weeks 4 days, which was a Thursday. My last day was the Friday before and I used vacation time that week. So I stopped 6 days before birth. I tried to cut my hours back a bit a couple weeks prior at my OB's request."

- "I dropped down to part-time a couple months prior but worked right up until I gave birth at 38 weeks."

- "My girls were born at 39 weeks 5 days and I stopped working 3 to 4 days before because it was the weekend and the Fourth of July holiday so the office was closed."

- "I stopped working just shy of 35 weeks and delivered at 37 weeks 2 days. I was fairly confident I'd make it to 37 weeks and just wanted a couple weeks off beforehand to rest."

- "I was in the hospital for 3 days around 33 weeks with steady contractions. We got them stopped and I went back to work the next week, and that was my last week! I worked until 34 weeks and had a C-section at 36 weeks."

PERFORMING WELL
AT WORK

With all that's going on with carrying or raising twins, it's pretty challenging to function at work, much less function well. Morning sickness and your physical constraints make it hard to concentrate and be at your best. The sleep deprivation and mental stress of balancing work and twins can take its toll.

That said, it's still possible to perform well at work and even enjoy your time there. How can you make sure your performance doesn't falter while at work?

Schedule appointments at convenient times

Think about all the people you need to set appointments with:

- Your doctor
- Your maternal-fetal medicine (MFM) specialist
- The twins' pediatrician

Schedule the earliest appointments so you can head to work right after, or use your sick or vacation time to go to your appointments. When you do, try to give your work enough notice so they can cover for you.

That said, your priority should always be you and your babies' health. In the end, work can wait. I came down with several complications that meant I had to see my doctors three times a week. You can't always predict or give your employer a clear timeline (and by that point, I was already on bed rest).

Don't complain to everyone at work

I'm all about sharing experiences with friends and co-workers. Still, be mindful of whom and how often you share gripes with. Not everyone will want to listen to your complaints, sadly. You also want to maintain professionalism and not make yourself look less capable.

You'll have better luck commiserating with fellow twin moms who've been there. Even fellow mom coworkers can't relate to the challenges of a twin pregnancy or raising twins. Online groups are great avenues for venting away without compromising your place at work.

Be efficient

The less time we have to waste, the more productive and efficient we can be. Handling work and either your pregnancy or twins takes a lot of effort. Focusing on the crucial actions you need to do allows you to work efficiently and effectively.

Define your "One Thing"

I had it all wrong. All this time, I thought having a to-do list was all I needed to be organized. Yes, a to-do list is better than not knowing what to do, but relying solely on a to-do list only adds things to do without asking whether any of it is important.

I read *The One Thing* by Gary Keller and Jay Papasan and it changed the way I view what I do during the day. Rather than just listing all the things you need to get done, ask yourself:

"What's the ONE thing you can do, such that by doing it everything else will be easier or unnecessary?"

Focus on the one "big" goal you want to get out of work, and do the one thing you can do right now to get you there.

Focus on work when you're at work

It can be difficult focusing on work with so much on your mind. You might worry about your twins or feel guilty about not seeing your babies during the day. You might even be distracted or start shopping online for baby stuff.

But these little distractions make your work day more difficult, especially if you have a lot to do. Slacking off of work can affect your performance. Not getting everything you needed to get done might mean you have to stay late or take work home.

Avoid those problems and work efficiently by focusing on work when you're at work. Create a new ritual, such as brewing a cup of tea or creating a to-do list the day before. Develop the discipline to work without distractions so you get your important tasks done.

Take frequent but planned breaks. Give yourself a set time to work on a project, then take that much-needed break to think about your twins. Plan to do bigger baby-related tasks during your lunch breaks. You're drawing clear lines to stay focused and get things done.

GOING BACK TO WORK AFTER
MATERNITY LEAVE

Let's jump forward and talk about the other half of work and twins: transitioning back after maternity leave. No matter how much time off you had or how your delivery went, going back to work is always a transition.

You'll learn:

- How to prepare for the first day back
- Flexible schedule arrangements to consider
- How to juggle being a working mom
- The ins and outs of pumping at work

How to prepare for the first day back

How you feel going back to work varies from mom to mom (and even from day to day). Some moms dread going back, while others welcome work as a much-needed time away from home. Regardless of how you feel, being prepared can make the transition back to work much smoother.

Start with a quick meeting with your employer

Get a recap of any changes that may have happened while you were gone. Ask which assignments or projects you'll tackle that first day back. Getting a sense of work before you actually come in to work can ease you back into your routine.

Pack everything the night before

As tired as you are the night before, you'll be even more tired in the morning. Get everything ready, from your outfit to your lunch. Get everything ready for the twins' day care or for the nanny.

Talk to HR about pumping arrangements

Email or call HR to find out about your pumping options. If your office has a room dedicated for pumping, ask them to leave the key at your desk so you don't have to wait for them to come in to work (in case you need to pump right away).

Go back to work mid-week

That way, you'll have a few days to adjust before the weekend.

Going back to work after maternity leave can be a bittersweet moment. You'll miss the twins but at the same time, might feel glad for the break. You have new responsibilities to fulfill, yet the old ones at home remain. By preparing in advance and getting your things in order with work, you can make the transition back to work seamless and smooth.

Working a flexible schedule

Ask most moms what makes them happy with their decision to work not, and you'll find a common factor. Surprisingly, it's not whether they work ("I love working and contributing in ways other than being a mom") or not ("I love being with my kids during the day"). It's flexibility.

Several factors might make you want to consider a flexible schedule. You might want to spend as much time as possible with your twins, or you want to save money and reduce your childcare needs. Maybe it's because you just want to avoid rush hour traffic. No matter your reasons, a flexible schedule may be right for you. Here are a few examples:

Work from home

When you work from home, you're doing the work you'd do in the office but from home. You can...

- **Work from home in the evenings.** Let's say you need to leave work by 4pm to pick up the twins from day care. You can finish your work by 4pm, pick them up, then finish your work in the evenings after they're in bed.

- **Work from home one day (or more) a week.** One of the flex schedules I've had was to work one day a week from home. You reduce your commute and office time by 20%.

- **Work from home completely.** Depending on your work, you can find or request an arrangement that allows you to work remotely 100%.

Shift your schedule earlier or later

Many people—parents or not—have a shifted schedule to avoid traffic. You can work either earlier in the day so you can leave early, or you can come in later and work later as well.

I had worked earlier and left earlier in the day. This allowed me to pick up my eldest from school and relieve the nanny by 4pm. You'd need to coordinate with someone, in my case my husband, to handle mornings.

Work part-time

Part-time work can be anything from reducing your hours all the way to 20 hours to just an hour less each day. Some examples of part-time work include:

- Working four days a week
- Working half days every day
- Leaving every day a few hours earlier
- Arriving to work every day a few hours later

Work odd hours

Some parents work a "graveyard shift" so their kids always have a parent with them. Some jobs need folks round the clock, so you might work 4pm to midnight, for instance.

Job share

A version of part-time, you and another employee would share the same duties and split one full-time job. For instance, you'd come in Monday to Wednesday and she'd come in Thursday and Friday, or you'd come in 9 to 1 and she'd come in 1 to 5. To the company, the same work gets done, split between two people.

Work four 10-hour days

Another way to enjoy a day off while still earning a full-time income is to condense your 40 hours in four days. Your days would be longer, but you'd have one day a week besides the weekends all to yourself.

Freelance or consult

And still another option is to freelance or consult for your current company. You'd no longer be an employee but a freelancer or consultant working your own hours. You'd lose benefits, but you'd work on your own time. You can either work completely from home or come in to the office when needed.

Is a flexible schedule right for you?

Two key factors make working a flexible arrangement possible. The first is your career capital: what are the rare and valuable skills that will give you leverage to shape the career you love? Every employee is replaceable, but the more valuable you are to your company, the easier it will be for you to shape a schedule that suits you.

The second is the right job. A flexible schedule might be more difficult to approve if your job requires daily meetings or collaborating with people on a constant basis.

But maybe you work independently and can be more creative alone, or you don't attend meetings regularly. Your employer would be more likely to approve a different schedule. Consider the type of work you have and see if your job will even enable you to create the schedule you desire.

How to ask for a flexible schedule

Phrase the request as a benefit to your company and boss.
Don't mention the benefits you reap with the new schedule.
However close you are with your bosses, they're still looking
out for themselves and the company. Imagine if your boss had
to explain to his boss or colleagues that you have a flexible
schedule because you wanted a better work-life balance—it just
wouldn't make him look good.

Instead, focus on the benefits that your boss and the company
can have. You might mention that the company can save money
with your reduced salary and benefits, or that you can be
available for "off hours" such as early mornings or late evenings
to cover work outside the typical nine-to-five schedule.

**Remind your boss about why this schedule works for your
job duties.** Bosses may feel hesitant to grant flexible work
arrangements because they fear the rest of the company will
follow suit, or that they would look like they're favoring you
above everyone else. Instead, highlight how your job is different
from others'. Explain how this schedule is doable with the type
of work you do, and mention how you can continue performing
well even with your new schedule.

Start by asking for the ideal schedule. While you don't want to
request something outrageous, ask for the schedule you'd love
to have within reason and let your boss negotiate down should
she need to. For instance, if you'd love to work part-time three
days a week, request it, even if you think a likelier solution
would be to work four days a week. You never know—your boss
just might agree to your request. If she doesn't, then let her
negotiate your request down.

Be flexible and open to suggestions. Your boss may not agree to everything you request, so be flexible. You can even ask for suggestions on what she thinks would work for her. If your boss is given the chance to craft a possible solution, she'll be more likely to agree to it if she feels like she contributed to the idea.

Offer solutions to any lingering doubts. Your boss will want to know you're actually doing work and not lying down on the couch watching TV. Give him a general schedule of when you'd be working. You can provide weekly progress reports. Should you need to meet face-to-face, suggest a Skype chat or offer to come in to the office for meetings. Make a list of the equipment and gadgets you have at home that will make working from home possible, such as high-speed Internet or computer programs.

Whichever work arrangement you're looking into, offer assurances to any possible doubts your boss might have. This not only helps strengthen your case, but it's a good exercise for yourself before bringing it up to see if your flexible schedule is even doable.

Agree to a trial run. Your boss might feel like she's getting the short end of the stick or that this schedule will make her work life more difficult. Give her an out so she doesn't feel like she's signing her life away by keeping the schedule open-ended.

Agree to a trial run, whether it's formal like a three month run or casual just to "see how it works out." Offer to meet down the line to discuss your schedule and tweak as needed. Your boss will feel like nothing is set in stone and can bring up any issues she sees.

Even though you're asking for a flexible schedule to improve your life, a truly successful arrangement is one where both parties come to a happy conclusion. You're not out to simply get as much as you can out of your work and leave them dry. Instead, find a schedule that works for both you and your employer.

Juggling being a working mom

Once you've returned to work for several days, you'll need to juggle your time as efficiently as possible. Many of my blog readers have asked me how I "do it all" when I worked full-time, raised kids, and ran a business.

The good news is, it gets easier, especially as your twins get older, but during those first few months, you might feel guilty, both at work and at home. You might find yourself scrambling to meet pick-up times and leaving work on time. For a standard 9-to-5 schedule, you might feel like you hardly get to see your twins in a single day.

These are the tips I share with working moms wondering how to get it all done.

Do things after the twins are asleep

Put off anything you can until after the twins are asleep. If you feel like you hardly see them, put off everything you normally do until after they're asleep. As they get older, doing things around the house with them in tow is easier. For now, save anything you don't need to do right this moment for later so you can spend time with the babies.

Stick to the absolute essentials, like putting your milk storage bags in the refrigerator. (Don't even worry about washing pump parts—stick those in the fridge for later.) Cook later in the evening. You won't feel like all the time you could be spending with the twins isn't only on doing chores.

Be picky with your time

Those of us who are most limited in time are forced to be picky with what we do with it. Without the hours we had before kids, we're left to doing the absolute essentials.

So, what should go on your picky list? Anything that's an absolute must. The kinds of tasks that would affect you and your family in a negative way if they weren't done. Also on that list are things that give you genuine enjoyment, like your hobbies or calling a friend.

Be efficient with your time

I don't really "do it all." I, like everyone else, have a finite 24 hours in the day—I need to be as efficient as possible with every minute of it.

Limit the distractions of your day so you use the hours you have as efficiently as possible. For instance:

- **Run errands** like going to the bank on the way home or on my lunch break.
- **Shop online,** where you can read reviews and save time from going to the store.

- **Keep meals simple.** You have a full pass to prepare the simplest of meals during the baby stage. I don't bother with recipes that take longer than an hour to cook.

- **Get organized.** Rely on to-do lists on your phone or physical planners.

Get your partner on board

If you have a partner, he needs to make the life changes necessary to accommodate your new family life. Maybe he wakes up earlier to prepare the milks and breakfast, or he comes home early to handle bath times so you're not alone. Maybe he can work from home a few days, or handle day care drop-offs.

Don't assume that childcare falls solely on your shoulders. Let your partner cover responsibilities as well so you're not delegating but parenting equally.

Hold realistic expectations

Be realistic about what to expect. It's not so much resigning to a life of messy homes, frozen dinners, or scrambling every minute. Instead, you're accepting this season in your life as it is, knowing it'll soon pass as all seasons do.

Make the moments count

Quality time isn't just about doing brain-enhancing or baby-bonding activities. Any time spent with your babies can be special—make the moments count. Reconnect with them while you nurse. Sing songs in the bath. Sneak cuddles when changing into pajamas.

Being with your twins is time you're with them, from changing diapers to stimulating activities. Quality doesn't depend on the amount of time you spend or the activities you do. Rather it's your intention and mindfulness when you're with them.

The ins and outs of pumping at work

As if breastfeeding didn't come with its own challenges, trying to keep your supply up away from home and your twins can be daunting. You're also dealing with the transition back to work after a challenging first few months with the babies. Yet even with all that, pumping at work—even if not your favorite task—is possible with a few, simple hacks to consider.

Contact your boss or HR before your first day back

Finding the lactation room or building a makeshift pumping area shouldn't fall on your shoulders on your first day back at work. Instead, inform your boss or HR staff about your plans to pump and what arrangements are in place to make that happen.

The pumping room should ideally have:

- a small refrigerator
- an extension cord for your pump (so you don't have to bend down to the floor each time)
- a table and comfortable chair
- a folding screen near the door to prevent accidental walk-ins

Pack the essentials

There's nothing worse than going to work and realizing you'd forgotten to pack your pump parts. Keep a list of these essential items to bring:

- **Your pump.** Carry your pump in a proper container so it doesn't break. You wouldn't carry your laptop in a tote bag, so don't subject your pump to a light-weight bag either.

- **The pump parts.** If you use Medela, bring a few extras of the white membranes and leave them at work.

- **Bottles or storage bags.** Bring enough for all your pump sessions.

- **Ice pack and bottle bag.** Keep your milk fresh by packing an ice pack and keeping the bottles in an insulated bottle bag.

- **Hands-free pumping bra.** This was one of those "How did I live without this before?" purchases. I used to just rely on my nursing tops or bras to keep the pumps in place, but later realized a hands-free bra is a must.

- **A breastfeeding cover.** Bring a breastfeeding cover or a large receiving blanket for extra privacy.

- **A smart phone, book, or magazine.** If you don't plan to rest or work during your pumping sessions, bring some form of entertainment to keep you occupied. You can also use your iPhone to set a timer or to look at photos or videos of your babies while you pump to help increase milk flow.

Pump efficiently

With a busy schedule, meetings galore, and people to deal with, working moms can find it difficult to squeeze in a pumping session. Treat your pumping sessions as work commitments. Schedule time blocks on your calendar and treat it like any other meeting.

You'll also want to pump about the same times your babies would normally have nursed with you so your body maintains the same schedule.

Try to pump at least 20 minutes for each breast, even if milk flow stops towards the end. Pumping even if no milk comes out signals to the body to produce even more.

Lastly, save time and use a double pump. Whether you rent or buy, get your hands on a double pump as this will halve the time you spend pumping.

HANDLING THE EXHAUSTION OF A TWIN PREGNANCY

If you've ever wondered whether it's normal to feel this tired in a twin pregnancy, more than likely, it is. The nausea and fatigue are unbearable. The weight of the pressure makes walking from one room to the next exhausting, and you'd rather stay parked on the couch than do anything else.

A twin pregnancy is no joke. It's one of those experiences where any complaints from a singleton pregnancy seems laughable in comparison.

Now more than ever do you need to listen to your body. The exhaustion won't go away entirely, but you can find ways to feel a little more comfortable. Neglect the warning signs and you run the risk of ignoring complications or making the pain and discomfort worse.

Here are my top tips on how to survive the exhaustion of a twin pregnancy:

Don't do crazy exercises

While you shouldn't be a sloth, you don't have to exercise as much with a twin pregnancy compared to a singleton one. Our bodies just have more complications to watch out for. Your best bet is to stick to moderate exercise and daily activity.

So, what does a moderate exercise plan look like? It'll depend on you and your discussion with your doctor, but more than likely, there won't be any push to exercise as vigorously as those in a singleton pregnancy. You can moderate your current workouts to be less intense, as well as shorter.

Above all, listen to your body. Too many complications can happen when we push ourselves beyond what our bodies can take. Err on the side of safety and stick to moderate exercise.

And if you can't or don't feel like exercising? No sweat, either.

Get a temporary disability placard

Apply for a temporary disability placard to hang in your car. You can park in disabled parking spots, saving you a ton of extra steps. From groceries to the doctor's office, you don't have to walk far from your car to the entrance. Such a lifesaver when, for many pregnant twin moms, walking a few steps is already a challenge.

Ask your doctor's office if they have application forms, or look for them online through your state's DMV. Your doctor will sign a form verifying that you do need the placard. Then you send it in the mail, and you'll get your placard in a few weeks.

Work less

I know, easier said than done. Especially when you're in your first trimester and you're not exactly keen on announcing the pregnancy yet to your coworkers.

Even if you can't avoid work long-term, try to take it easy. Don't stay later than you need to, or volunteer for time-consuming activities. Ask for a random day off periodically just to rest at home.

And when you're further along in your pregnancy, talk with your doctor about how comfortable you feel coming to work. Many pregnant twin moms stop working, work from home, or go on bed rest around 28 to 32 weeks.

Check your iron

Even though feeling tired is normal, it's still good practice to discuss your energy levels with your doctor. One thing in particular to do is to check your iron levels. Unusual fatigue is a symptom of low iron levels.

Most prenatal vitamins include iron, but twin pregnancies need extra. A quick check will clue you in on whether your exhaustion is due to low iron.

Take care of yourself

Along with toning down exercise, you can do so much to take care of yourself. You can...

- **Drink one gallon of water per day.** Yup, one gallon. It sounds insane and it is when you actually measure and see how much less of it you're currently drinking.

- **Take hourly breaks.** Try not to stay in one activity for longer than an hour. If you're at your desk at work, stand up for a minute to give your body a break.

- **Make rest a priority.** Don't feel guilty for resting or that you have to justify taking a nap when there's still so much to do. Your body is making two babies! You can't see it from the outside, but your body is doing enough work to burn 600 extra calories a day. That's a lot of work!

Do one thing a day

Cook dinner, turn in preschool forms, deposit a check... your to-do list never seems to end, and those are just daily things, not even twin-related tasks.

No wonder you're tired.

Try to limit your tasks to just one thing a day. When you have no energy left and can hardly walk, do just one thing and be okay with it. It's really fine to disrupt your normal routine during this season in your life. You're not your usual self right now and probably won't be for a few more months. Find ways to do less and pick just one thing to do each day.

Feeling tired from a twin pregnancy is inevitable. There's no magic pill or secret sauce to make fatigue go away, especially as you near your third trimester.

Still, there's hope, even if they come in little things that add up and make the day a tad more bearable than before. Taking care of yourself to avoid further complications. Pacing yourself so you're not doing too much.

It's normal to feel tired, but by doing the above tips, you'll get through the day with a little more energy and patience and a lot less fatigue.

SECTION 7:
PREPARING FOR A TWIN DELIVERY

UNDERSTANDING
LABOR WITH TWINS

If only we knew exactly when and how labor will happen. Not only is labor different in so many ways, but as twin moms, we also have unique circumstances to consider. The best we can do is educate ourselves about the most common and likely scenarios.

With twins, especially with high-risk twins, delivery becomes even more unexpected. You could be in your doctor's office when she announces you're delivering that day, or find yourself nearing 38 weeks counting down the days until you're able to deliver.

Let's begin this chapter with common symptoms of labor to watch out for. Then I'll share best practices for laboring at home.

Labor symptoms to look out for

Regardless of your symptoms, you'll need to time how often you experience them. Use an app on your phone or even paper and pen to track when your contractions start and end. True onset of labor is best determined by its rhythmic pattern.

Below are a few symptoms to look out for:

Tightening in the uterus

Braxton Hicks feels like a painless, mild tightening in your uterus and can happen as early as the second trimester. They're "practice contractions"—your uterus is tightening to prepare for labor. Some women experience this while others don't at all.

If you feel a tightening in your uterus, see if it's Braxton Hicks or the real onset of labor. Braxton Hicks contractions are irregular and come and go at erratic times.

To rule out Braxton Hicks as the cause for the contractions, you'll want to:

- Lay on your left side so your blood is better able to flow with less pressure.
- Walk slowly around the room.
- Drink water.

Track the contractions as well and see if there's a pattern. If so, and if after doing the above and you're still experiencing contractions, you're likely entering labor.

Cramps

Another symptom of labor women feel is cramps. This is like the cramps you might feel during your menstrual cycle. If you feel abdominal pain and cramps, again, track when and how often they happen. Then, try the following to see if doing so relieves the discomfort:

- Change positions.
- Drink water.

- Place a warm compress on the area that's cramping.
- Soak in a warm bath.

If doing those doesn't relieve discomfort, and you see a pattern to your cramps, you're likely in labor.

Pelvic pressure and backache

Like cramps, you might feel pelvic pressure or even backache as you begin labor. Baby A might be dropping into position closer to your cervix and causing the pelvic pressure, causing you to feel extra weight in your pelvic region.

If you feel this as well as backache, you're likely in the first stages of labor.

Constipation and gas

Some symptoms disguise themselves well, such as through constipation and gas. You might feel like you have to poop and can't seem to push anything out, or you feel gassy, like you have to pass gas. These can be so mild you might think drinking prune juice will relieve the discomfort.

Instead, these can be the first symptoms of labor. If the gas pains and constipation persist, begin timing them to track how often they happen. If you see a pattern, you're likely in labor.

Water breaking

A small percentage of women experience their water breaking. Your babies are inside an amniotic sac, and when that membrane ruptures, the amniotic fluid leaks out. This is what we call your water breaking and is a sign of labor.

Discuss with your doctor her protocol on what to do when your water breaks. Usually, you won't need to head to the hospital just yet. You'll want to labor at home until your contractions are a certain pattern apart, but note the time it happened, since you'll likely need to deliver within 24 hours of your water breaking.

How to labor at home

You'll likely be home during the early stages of labor. This is when your contractions are rhythmic, but still too far apart and too short to need to be in the hospital. Usually a hospital will admit you if your cervix has dilated to 3 centimeters. Your doctor will tell you how many minutes apart your contractions should be before you go to the hospital.

What should you do in the meantime?

- **Rest.** Your body will go through tough physical challenges in a few hours—it's best to reserve your energy for then. Try to sleep or take a nap, especially if your symptoms happen at night.

- **Do last-minute preparations.** By now you should have your hospital bag ready, but you might still need to add last-minute things you couldn't do before. Start packing these items or prepare your home for leaving.

- **Eat and drink water.** Staying hydrated during labor is important, so make sure to drink water. Eat as well, since you probably won't eat anything once you're in the hospital. Stick to easily digested and high-energy food , as well as simple soups and broths.

- **Breathe through your contractions.** Each contraction will likely feel more intense and longer than the previous one. Breathe through these using exercises you learned from a birthing class or your doctor. Remaining calm and relaxed even during contractions reduces discomfort.

- **Call your babysitter.** If you have older children, make arrangements with a babysitter to drive to your home. Give them enough time to head over but not so much time that you don't really need them there just yet. Long before labor happens, ask them to have their overnight bag ready to go so they're packed and ready to come over.

WHAT TO EXPECT WITH A
TWIN DELIVERY

In many ways, a twin delivery follows the same protocol as a singleton one. You'll follow the same instructions on when to drive to the hospital. Your doctor will be with you to deliver the twins, and you'll likely stay the same amount of days at the hospital, barring any complications.

But in many other ways, a twin delivery needs to be treated differently than if you were delivering just one. Let's talk about what to expect when you deliver the twins.

C-section or vaginal?

According to the Centers for Disease Control and Prevention, 75% of twin deliveries are via C-section as of 2008. The rates are higher than singleton pregnancies because of potential complications. The mother's health and two babies in the womb also contribute to this number. With two babies in different positions, often a C-section is needed to deliver.

Discuss your options with your doctor. Ask what conditions need to be in place to have a vaginal delivery as well as those that would need a C-section. Often, a vaginal delivery is possible if:

- **Baby A is head down.** Ideally both babies will be head down, but even if Baby B isn't, your doctor might try to either turn the baby head down, or deliver him breech.

- **Baby A is bigger.** It'd be pretty tough for Baby B to be delivered vaginally if he's the bigger of the two.

- **Both babies have their own placentas.** If the twins share a placenta, you'll likely need a C-section. It'd be dangerous to deliver Baby A and the placenta before Baby B came out.

- **You and your babies are healthy.** The health of your twins as well as yours need to be considered when deciding whether to deliver by C-section or vaginally.

Each doctor has her own requirements and protocols. Discuss the factors that would lead to one decision or another.

In some cases, you may have a "mixed delivery." You might deliver Baby A vaginally, then deliver Baby B by C-section. This happens because of complications or the baby's position.

The best thing you can do for yourself is to prepare for any possibility. You may have expectations of your birth experience, but being open shifts the focus from your expectations to having healthy babies. Even if you don't plan to have a C-section, be open to the possibility that it might happen. Your goal isn't to have a particular birth, but to have the safest and healthiest delivery.

Delivering in the operating room

You'll likely deliver in the operating room, even if you're having a vaginal delivery. With twins, complications can arise at any time. Should they need to operate on you at any point, it's more sensible to already be in the operating room.

Delivering in the operating room, even if vaginally, may not be your ideal experience. After all, you're dealing with bright lights and a cold, sterile room, but your and the twins' safety is top priority during delivery. Doctors want to make sure they're ready to respond to any situation.

Once the twins are born and assessed, they'll transfer you to your own bed and maybe even your own room. You'll get to spend a ton of time bonding with your little ones in a much cozier environment soon after.

Another thing to watch out for? Around delivery time, there's a chance you'll have the chills and your body will shake. If so, expect a lot of trembling and teeth-chattering, as if you're outside in the snow with no jacket. This is your hormones changing combined with body temperature. Don't freak out or think something is wrong—it's totally normal!

Who will be in the delivery room?

A typical singleton delivery doesn't usually involve too many people. With my eldest, I had a total of four people with me: my doctor, a nurse, my mom, and my husband.

But a twin delivery involves more people, regardless of how you deliver. My doctor gave me a heads up that there'd be a ton of people, and she was right. If your delivery is anything like mine, it might include your doctor, a resident doctor, nurses, multiple NICU pediatric doctors (I had four for each baby), an anesthesiologist and your partner.

These folks will be working hard and fast to ensure a safe and healthy delivery for your twins. It'll be a crowded room, but it's nice to know you're taken care of and are in good hands.

How to cope with a C-section

Some C-sections are planned, such as early signs that a vaginal delivery isn't possible, or maybe you've already had a C-section with your older child and will do so again with the twins. Even scheduled, you still might have an emergency C-section sooner than expected.

The good news is, many moms have admitted that their C-sections weren't as bad as they thought. Some report that they had little pain and minimal bleeding. Every experience is different, but just know that a C-section doesn't always have to be the worst.

How to prepare for a possible C-section

A C-section recovery can be more challenging because you're healing from an incision. Since many C-sections aren't planned, do keep these tips in mind:

- **Leave heavy lifting to someone else**, or long before your pregnancy has progressed. A C-section recovery prohibits you from heavy lifting, especially with your incision. Instead, ask others to do household chores or heavy lifting for you.

- **Pack "granny underwear."** Find loose-fitting, high-waist underwear that won't rub on your incision. To top it off, wear loose dresses or yoga pants or leggings with high waists. Some pants might rub on the incision, even if your underwear doesn't.

- **Speak with others who've had a C-section.** In some birthing classes, C-sections are just a small topic that gets touched on. Find other moms for best tips on recovering from a C-section.

Best practices to recover from a C-section

Once you've had your C-section, what are some of the best ways to recover and get you back on your feet?

- **Walk.** C-section moms are adamant about the benefits of walking after a C-section. Without overdoing it and always listening to your body, walk around your hospital floor. The walking will help your incision heal and prevent your body from being too inactive. Even it's uncomfortable, tell your nurses to help you walk around the floor.

- **Take pain medication if needed.** Some moms might be wary of pain relief pills as part of their recovery, but keep in mind that nurses monitor your use and prescribe only the amount you need. It's also not a long-term solution—you're only expected to take medication during recovery and when your body needs it most. Track your medicine in a notebook so you don't forget when you last took a dose.

- **Visit your babies often** while you're still in the hospital and they're in the NICU. Even though you may feel tired or in pain, holding and spending time with your twins will help.

- **Ask for help.** As you did before giving birth, ask others to help with household chores like laundry, cooking, and cleaning. You'll need to rest as much as possible, even with your newborn twins at home.

WHAT TO DO AFTER THE
TWINS ARE BORN

The next few hours and days after giving birth to your twins will be a whirlwind.

Bonding with your twins

You might feel worried that you won't be able to bond with your twins as much as you would've with one baby. You're torn from meeting one baby's needs to the next, and it's hard to focus on each one when they both need you so much.

Here's the thing though: bonding is a mindset—you *can* bond with each twin, right from the start. Bonding doesn't need hours of uninterrupted time. It happens in the simplest and even smallest of moments.

Don't feel like you missed your opportunity to bond if complications arise or you can't hold them. Your twins will love you regardless of how they were born or how soon after you were able to hold them. Work with your hospital staff to balance your preferences and health and safety needs.

What happens after you deliver

Immediately after delivery, your doctor will likely show you your twins as they come out. They'll suction their noses and mouths to allow for air to pass. Your doctor might place the first baby on you to maintain your baby's temperature. All this time, they're observing each baby and giving them an Apgar score. They'll asses each baby's:

- Skin color
- Heart rate
- Reflexes
- Muscle tone
- Breathing rate and effort

Soon after, the NICU pediatricians will assess each baby for a few minutes. As a twin mom, your pregnancy is a high-risk one. It's important for doctors to check your twins after birth so they can take action. They'll also give any necessary medications.

More than likely, your partner will hold Baby A while Baby B makes his grand entrance. He'll go through the same procedures as Baby B. If you've had a C-section, your partner and the doctors will handle the twins while you get stitched up.

Whether you'll hold your twins right away or not depends on your doctor, the procedures, and any complications, but if you're able to hold them, try to have skin-to-skin contact. The world will be a new and scary place for your twins. They need to hear your familiar heartbeat, so I encourage you to hold them close to your heart. Since they've heard your voice (and your partner's), talk to them as well. They'll feel reassured with a familiar sound.

Breastfeeding after delivery

One of the best ways to bond with your twins is through breastfeeding. If you're both ready and willing, the minutes after giving birth are a great time to start. Your babies will be alert and awake, so it's a good time to introduce them to your breast.

Don't worry if they don't take to sucking right away or feel like they're going to starve if they don't nurse right away (they won't!). Instead, use the time to get to know your babies. Talk to them, stroke their faces, or hold and look at them.

In the hospital, you can either tandem nurse your twins or nurse one at a time. You can use your twin nursing pillow or the nurses can help prop pillows on either side. Ask the nurses, doctors, or lactation consultants to show you how to tandem nurse. Many hospitals include consultants to help you nurse, whether you feed tandem or not.

With tandem nursing, you'll be holding your twins in a football hold. Each baby lays on either side of you with their mouths latched on each breast and their feet pointing to your back. They call it football hold because it's similar to the way a football player would grasp a ball as he's running. Your hands will cradle your twins' heads while your forearms will support their bodies. Tandem nursing keeps the twins on the same schedule.

Or you can nurse your twins one at a time if you prefer. This might give you a better grasp if you're worried about holding tiny newborn bodies. You might also prefer nursing individually to spend one-on-one time with each baby. It might take more time, but at least you're only dealing with one baby at a time.

Even if you're nursing one at a time, try to maintain the same schedule for your twins. You'll want to nurse Baby A, for instance, then right away nurse Baby B.

Monitoring your health (and your twins)

Your recovery

Once you're in the recovery room, nurses will continue to check your health and your twins. Constant interruptions are tough with the hospital staff checking in on you. It's important they do, though, in case you run into complications.

A day after giving birth, I summoned a nurse to help me go to the restroom when she noticed unusual bleeding. It turned out I had blood clots that the doctors needed to remove immediately. One nurse helping me to the bathroom turned into eight people in my room removing the clots as quickly as possible.

You'll likely have nurses checking for things like your uterus size and your blood flow. They'll also monitor everything about your health, from blood pressure to your temperature, coming in and out giving you pain medication and your meals.

Monitoring your twins

Besides your health, nurses will be checking your twins round the clock. In some cases, like in mine, nurses run hourly tests on your twins. They check for breathing, sugar levels, bowel movements, and maintaining their temperature. They'll also run exams on your babies' hearing and eyesight and other bodily functions.

Some moms prefer to be with their twins through every test. Others would rather the twins stay in the nursery for a few hours. This is up to you and can even change from one day to the next. With my eldest, he stayed in our room the entire time, and either my husband or I would go to the nursery for any tests, but my twins stayed in the nursery a few hours at a time since they needed to run more tests than usual.

Also, most babies lose weight a few days after birth before regaining the weight again. Don't freak out if your twins lose anywhere from 5-10% of their body weight over the first few days. They'll regain the weight over the next several days.

Your twins' pediatrician

Your twins' pediatrician will likely visit you on the first day they're born. She'll assess their health, including their weight and growth. You might need to schedule appointments with her or other specialists. For instance, you might need to run blood tests a few days after birth to monitor jaundice levels.

What to do about visitors at the hospital

Your family and friends might want to visit you and the twins at the hospital. Whether you have large families or small, you may wonder how you'll handle visitors. Maybe you're considering not inviting them at all. You feel overwhelmed with the emotions of having birth, or you want to bond as a family. Maybe you need to heal. Keeping visitors manageable is key. Here are a few options to consider.

Have a no visitors rule

At least until you go home with the twins. You might want to use the time at the hospital to learn as much as you can from the nurses. You'll likely need to heal and relax, and of course, get to know the babies.

Invite only a select few

Maybe that's your parents or close friends—people you wouldn't consider having to entertain. They can provide much needed support and a refreshing welcome from the outside world. They can also help cover shifts in case your partner needs to run an errand or drive home.

Set visiting hours

For some parents, an extended NICU stay can make your hospital stay lonely. Balance the number of visitors and establish visiting hours with your friends and family. You can even let the nurses know so they can be the "bad guy" who tells your visitors they can't come in just yet.

You may crave social interaction with familiar faces. You'll likely want to have visitors come and keep you company. Each family is different. Focus on your needs and those of your new family. Everyone else will understand!

Post-delivery paperwork and tasks

Before leaving the hospital, you'll need to handle some paperwork and tasks, including:

Birth certificates

At the hospital, you'll supply your twins' information and apply for birth certificates. The hospital will mail the application and you'll receive the certificates in the mail. In the meantime, you'll get a temporary record of the information as well as a confirmation stating you applied. While you can always change names later, it's a good idea to have them picked out ahead of time. At least have a few contenders so you're ready to name the babies before you leave.

Social security numbers

Along with the birth certificate is the option to apply for social security numbers for your twins. You'll do this at the hospital at the same time you submit the birth certificate information.

Your employer

You don't need to do this right from the hospital, but it's a good idea to let your employer know you've given birth. Contact either your boss or HR department so they can add your twins to your insurance provider. You'll likely have up to 30 days to add or remove your twins to your insurance plan.

SURVIVING A
NICU STAY

The NICU, or neonatal intensive-care unit, specializes in ill or premature babies. Because over half of twins are born premature, many are also likely to need time in the NICU. The reasons vary, from needing help with processing sugar to maintaining body temperature. The NICU staff are skilled professionals who help babies grow well enough to go home.

For some, NICU is expected, while for others, it comes as a surprise. Your twins can be admitted to the NICU:

- While you're still pregnant. If your twins are high-risk, your doctor may have already told you they'll likely be admitted to the NICU.

- Before an emergency C-section.

- After being examined post-delivery.

As overwhelming as it may be to have your twins in the NICU, know that you're not alone. So many parents have gone through the NICU and now have thriving, happy twins at home. In this chapter, you'll learn about a typical stay in the NICU and how it impacts you and your family. You'll get practical tips on how to make the most of your NICU time, and learn how to stay motivated when you feel burned out.

A typical day at the NICU

Each time you visit the NICU, you'll need to "scrub in." This includes washing your hands and forearms with antibacterial soap for a set time. The staff does this as well. The extra precaution is to keep germs away from the NICU as much as possible.

Then, you'll make your way to your twins and check in with the nurses and doctors. They'll fill you in on their stats, such as how many ounces they're eating or their bilirubin count. Next, you'll spend time with the babies.

They'll feed most likely every three hours, either by nursing, bottle, or through a tube. You may also use this time to pump and help with diaper changes. The majority of your time will be spent holding, snuggling, and bonding with your twins. You'll also want to do skin-to-skin contact when you're in the NICU whenever possible.

Practical tips for your NICU stay

You're in the middle of a whirlwind of emotions and dealing with your twins' extended stay. Below are practical tips to make the process as smooth as possible.

Tour the NICU

If you know your twins will be born early, take a tour of the NICU to get familiar with the process and the environment. Talk with doctors about complications your twins might face and how to best cope with them.

Include your other children

Not all hospitals allow children to visit, but if yours does, do include your child. Bringing her to the NICU will help her bond with her baby siblings.

Gather a support system of family and friends

These folks will be your village and will help with caring for your older children and your household. They'll also provide much-needed morale and help with anything you're too busy to handle. Coordinate how to care for your older kids, such as school pickups or preparing dinner.

Speak with other moms whose children were in the NICU

No one knows what it feels like to have babies in the NICU other than those who've gone through it. Connect with other moms, whether those you know or online in our Facebook group. Ask them to share their biggest surprises, their emotions, and how they best coped with this time.

What to bring to the NICU

- **Your pump.** If your twins have difficulty latching, you can provide breast milk with your pump. At home, pump every three hours and bring the supply to the NICU each day. Some hospitals may even have a pump rental you can use so you won't have to bring yours with you.

- **A notebook.** Use your notebook to write any questions you may have for the doctors or nurses. You can also record information such as their stats or when they go off oxygen and feeding tubes.

- **Snacks and a water bottle.** Bring snacks so you don't have to run out to get food all the time. You might get tired of hospital or cafeteria food.

- **A pillow and blanket.** NICU rooms are usually cold, so an extra blanket can make your stay more comfortable. You might even want to bring a pillow in case you want to nap.

- **Headphones.** If the beeps and alarms wake you up or make you feel anxious, wear headphones to block them.

How to stay motivated

Having your twins admitted to the NICU takes a toll on your emotions. You feel like it's never going to end, especially when just a few days turns into weeks. You'll need to adjust to a new routine that includes driving to the hospital each day. You feel guilty no matter where you are. At home, you feel like you should be at the hospital with the twins. At the hospital, you feel like you should be home with your older child.

It can be scary and emotional to see tubes and machines, or you worry over every little "beep" from their monitors. If you have older children, you're also trying to maintain a normal life for her. Here's how to cope and stay motivated:

Trust that they're in good hands

The NICU staff is trained for helping babies grow and get well. Communicate with them often to answer any questions you may have. Know that each day brings them closer to when they can come home. It can be frustrating to feel stuck at the hospital. Believe that you will bring the babies home healthy and happy.

Take plenty of photos and videos

While you can't bring them home, you can rely on photos and videos to watch. Share them with your older children as well as family and friends. Use Skype or FaceTime to chat with your children at home.

Focus on what you can do

One of the reasons an NICU stay is so difficult is because you feel helpless. It almost becomes a waiting game, with you feeling like you can't do anything about the outcome. Except you can! Focus on things you can do to help with the process, like pumping, taking notes, calling the nurses for updates throughout the day, and spending skin-to-skin contact time with your babies.

Be involved in their care

Be involved in their care as early as possible so it'll be a smoother transition when you go home. As hard as it is to leave your babies, use this time without them to heal from delivery before they come home with you. Staying busy can also help you channel your thoughts to more productive tasks instead of worrying about things you can't do.

Let go of the guilt

Don't beat yourself up about things you can't do. We all do the best we can, and no one is judging you because you missed a feeding or didn't spend as many hours as you wanted at the NICU.

Some of us who had a chance to carry all the way to 38 weeks might feel guilty because we delivered earlier. No matter how many times people tell you it was out of your hands, it's still easy to assume so much guilt because they arrived early. *Maybe if I just did this, or didn't do that*, you might tell yourself.

We all have expectations of our pregnancy and delivery, some of which may not happen. You are doing all you can. Your twins needing NICU time isn't your fault. Let go of the guilt and instead focus your energy into the excitement of welcoming them home.

Find support

Talk to your partner, family, and friends often. Cry if need be. Your emotions will feel intense—having someone to share those with can relieve the burden. Rely on the nurses for an extra boost during the bad days.

They're in good hands

Finally, remind yourself they're where they need to be. Taking your babies home before they're ready means more complications down the line. Their stay during the NICU will help them grow and stabilize. Each day at the NICU just means they're growing well enough to come home with you.

A stay in the NICU is never ideal for any twin mom, but you'll have the means to remain strong, productive, and positive throughout. Your fellow twin moms have gone through it and so

SURVIVING A NICU STAY

will you. They're raising happy and healthy twins, something to remember during the initial days when the unknown can feel so scary.

TOP TWIN ADVICE
FROM FELLOW TWIN MOMS

If you're like me, you didn't know a whole lot of twin moms when you first began your journey. Finding resources, support, and advice about twins can be difficult.

Below are the top pieces of advice your fellow twin moms want to share with you.

Be flexible

Having twins is so unpredictable! Just when you thought you had a plan, your twins take you on a different direction.

As a twin mom, you'll need to be flexible and open to any circumstances that may come your way. Your delivery might not be what you expected. Your twins' personalities can be so different from yours.

But be present and flexible and let go of past assumptions. It'll help you be more patient and understanding when things don't go according to plan.

Prepare in advance

Juggling two babies isn't easy. Your best bet is to prepare as much as possible in advance. For instance,

- Get all your gear ready before they arrive. Test and practice your strollers, car seats, and other baby gear.

- During bath time, lay out their pajamas before bath so you'll have everything ready once they're finished.

- During feeding time, gather all the things you'll need near you. That way, you won't need to get up for a burp cloth or your phone.

- Replenish diaper bags when you get home, not before you have to leave.

Being prepared will help you avoid some of the hassles of dealing with two babies at the same time.

Sync your twins' schedules

Singleton moms can get away with following their babies' schedules, but twin moms need to get both babies on the same schedule.

Let's say you want your babies to nap from 12pm to 1pm, but Baby A wakes up at 12:30 and Baby B is still sleeping. Try to put Baby A back to sleep a little bit longer, but if Baby A still won't sleep, then wake Baby B at 1pm as a compromise.

Here's another example: let's say both babies napped from 12pm to 1pm and Baby A wakes up first to feed. Even if it looks like Baby B can sleep longer, wake him up at 1pm as well so you can feed at the same time. Synchronize them so you don't have two schedules to track.

Establish a routine

Having a routine means doing the same things in the same sequence at generally the same times of the day.

You might have routines for bedtime, bath time, and feedings.

- Routines help your twins know what to expect next, even at this young age! They'll learn that a dark room means it's bedtime, and that waking up from a nap usually means getting milk.

- Routines will also help you plan your day without having to invest too much time into it. You'll run on automatic since you're doing the same things at the same time.

Invite the twins into your life

Twin parents sometimes feel like their lives are on hold because they have twins. In the early days, this is true. Your former lifestyle is on hold because you're now in the season of caring for newborn twins.

But don't be afraid to include the twins in your life, too.

For instance, it's okay to fold laundry while your twins are laying on a blanket next to you. You don't need to wait until they're asleep or someone is with you to fold clothes. Include the twins in the activity by playing peek-a-boo with their clothes, or talk to them about the colors of the onesies you're folding.

Inviting the twins into your life will not only save you time, but integrate your twins into family life.

Accept help

Now more than ever do you need to rely on your village. Accept help from anyone who expresses interest in pitching in.

Different ways people can help include:

- Bringing you a meal and holding the baby while you nap.
- Sleeping over and helping with routines.
- Caring for the twins so you can sleep at night.
- Playing with your older children.
- Doing household chores.

Be patient with your twins AND yourself

It's too easy to lose your patience with your twins. Each missed nap feels like a failure. You don't understand why they won't just latch already, and you're frustrated when they're inconsolable during an outing in the stroller.

When the tough times arrive—and they will—be patient

with your twins. They're adjusting to this new world just as much as you. Draw as much patience as you can, taking a quick break if needed.

And be kind to yourself. You are just as human as the next person. You're prone to frustration and emotions you're afraid to admit. You're just as tired with the lack of sleep. You will do fantastic, even if it may not seem like it at first.

Do what works for you

This is my mantra not just with twins but with anything parenting. I can tell you what works for me, and so can so many other twin moms.

Take the advice that seems to work, and filter those that don't. Each family is different. Each baby is different. Don't feel pressured that you're not following common advice or that something isn't working.

You're doing what works for you and your twins—and that's all that matters in the end.

SECTION 8:
CARING FOR TWINS

ESTABLISHING
ROUTINES

You may have heard it from other twin moms: get your twins on a routine. A schedule. Find a way to structure your day to make it easier for yourself and your twins.

But how?

If you already have an older child, you know how beneficial a routine can be for kids. So you can imagine how much more necessary a routine and schedule will be for your twins.

But what are routines and schedules, exactly? In this chapter, I want to share how both are important for structuring your day.

So, what's a routine? A routine is doing the same things around the same time in the same sequence.

Lots of sameness there, but bear with me.

You'll hear people talk about a bedtime routine, or a bath time routine, or a meal time routine. Each of those periods in the day include a series of things you do over and over.

But what about newborns? You might wonder. Newborns and babies benefit and thrive from routines just as much asi, if not more so than, older children.

Why routines are important

As overwhelming as welcoming twins can be, we forget just how confusing it can be for our twins as well. All this time, they've been cocooned in your womb with little change to their days. They didn't know night from day, or when to eat, or even that other people exist.

To go from that environment to ours is a big change.

So we help them along by bringing regularity into their lives. We make things as predictable as possible.

Your babies respond well to cues in their environment. They learn that darkness usually means sleep, and that laying on a mat means play. While they can't communicate as well as you and I do, they can learn to expect a certain rhythm to their days.

And we help them do that with routines.

Routines are also important for *you*. Think about all the things you do right now on autopilot. You have a morning routine of waking up, using the bathroom, then washing your face. After that, you put on your contacts, apply lotion to your face, and head to the kitchen for breakfast.

You do all these things in the same sequence without thinking about them too much. This saves you a ton of mental energy and time than, say, switching things up every morning. Consistency allows you to focus on other things that may need your full attention.

When your twins arrive, your routine will benefit you in the same way. You won't have to think about what's coming up next, or whether you feed them first or put them down for a nap. Because of your routine, you'll know without thinking too much about what to do next.

Routines are two-part:

- **Routines are the structure of your day.** With babies, this revolves around eating, sleeping, and being awake. They're like markers that segment your day into chunks and categories.

- **Routines are sequences of things you do** within each of those chunks. So within the sleeping part of your day, you have a series of little activities you do each time your twins sleep.

Routines as the structure for your day

When you think of routine, you might think of activities you do by the clock. Maybe you wake up every morning at 6am, eat lunch at 12pm and take a shower at 8pm. All these activities depend on the clock.

With your twins, however, think of routines as more like rhythms or flows to your day. One follows the previous activity instead of following the clock.

You won't put your newborn twins to nap at 9am and eat at 11am every day. Instead, you'll base nap time from how long it's been since they woke up for the day. You won't always feed them at 11am no matter what, but whenever they both wake up. That could be 11am, or it could be 11:30am.

How do you go about structuring your day with two babies?

Use the Eat-Awake-Sleep rhythm I learned from the book, *The Baby Whisperer* by Tracy Hogg.

It's much easier to feed your twins after they wake up, not before. It seems silly to do it this way, when, after all, babies fall asleep so easily and quickly from feeding. The sucking motion is a comfort, and with a full belly, it seems obvious to feed your twins to sleep.

The problem is that they'll start to rely on feeding and only feeding to fall asleep. Set them up with good habits by allowing them to fall asleep without feeding. Instead, give them milk after they wake up.

Giving them milk when they wake up also provides them energy to tackle their awake time. They're more alert and ready to stay awake with the energy they just consumed after waking up.

So here's an example cycle for newborn twins:

- Wake up for the day
- Eat
- Awake time
- Nap
- Eat
- Awake time
- Nap
- Eat
- Awake time
- Nap
- Eat
- Awake time
- Bath time

- Final feeding
- Bedtime

See a pattern? And notice I didn't put any times, or even how long each nap or awake time should be. Your situation will be different. One morning, your twins might only be able to handle an hour of awake time instead of their typical hour and a half. A nap can go for as long as three hours, while another lasts for an hour. You might have four or five short naps throughout the day instead of three.

You're basing their routine more on what had just happened.

However, a few areas where you *should* watch the clock are:

- **Awake time:** Generally, newborns should only be awake for an hour or an hour and a half at most at a time. If it's been an hour and a half, it's worth a shot to put your twins to nap.

- **Bath and bedtime:** Stick to a consistent bath and bedtime every night. Your twins might nap anywhere from four to five times in a day. Adjust their naps and awake time so they can take a bath and sleep for the night at the same time.

After all this talk about consistency and routine, here's a final bit of advice about this topic: it's okay to be flexible too.

Sometimes we focus so much on getting it right that we beat ourselves up if things don't go as planned, but guess what: your twins won't always nap in two-hour chunks. They might skip naps completely, or they'll nurse longer than you anticipated.

The consistency of your routine will cushion any unexpected changes that pop up. So don't feel bad if your twins won't nap or you stayed later than you anticipated at a friend's house. You and your twins will adjust, thanks to the consistency of your routine.

Routine as a sequence of activities

Next, let's talk about how to use routines as sequences.

Along with the familiarity of the general flow of your day comes the same things you do within each chunk. There are countless ways to create different routines—your routine will be unique to you and your family, and this will change once you meet your twins, but here are a few examples you can try:

Bath time routine

Here's a typical bath time routine with two adults. Once you get the hang of bath time, it's possible to do this alone. For the first few weeks, though, try to get as much help as you can.

1. Lay out the twins' sleepwear, from onesies to pajamas to swaddles. Have the diapers ready to go.

2. Fill the infant tub. Have the washcloth, bath soap, and towel nearby.

3. Undress and bathe Baby A while your partner undresses Baby B.

4. Hand Baby A to your partner to dry and dress.

5. Refill the infant tub and grab a new washcloth and towel.

6. Pick up and bathe Baby B.

7. Hand Baby B to your partner to dry and dress.

Sticking to the same bath time routine makes it much easier on you to know what's next.

Bedtime routine

For every set of twins is a unique bedtime routine just for them. Still, many bedtime routines are a mix of the following activities conducive for sleep. Your routine can include:

- Bath
- Changing into nighttime pajamas
- Reading books
- Playing a song on a mobile
- Holding a special blankie
- Singing nursery songs
- Saying good night to things in the room
- Wearing a swaddle
- Using a pacifier
- Nursing or feeding
- Turning on white noise
- Drawing the curtains and turning off the lights

Following the same routine can be a comfort for your twins to prepare them for a night of sleep.

Your nap time routine can be a simplified version of your bedtime routine. You might want to do most of the things you do, but drop the bath, or read one book instead of four, but the same idea is true for naps: do the same sequence of things so your twins know it's time for sleep.

PUTTING YOUR
TWINS TO SLEEP

Sleep.

It seems like you won't ever have enough of it. You can't seem to get your twins to do it. When you combine naps in the day with wake-ups at night, you realize why so many twin moms struggle with sleep.

It's amazing how getting your twins to sleep becomes the biggest issue those first few months. Newborns sleep 16 to 17 hours a day. When you see it that way, it sure feels like all babies do is sleep and you're coasting right along.

Except, unlike you and me, your twins won't sleep in long stretches, at least not the eight hours we're used to. You might get a five-hour stretch (I think I got *one* of those), but for the most part, babies nap in sporadic spurts.

This means lots of short stretches of sleep, throughout the day and night. They might sleep for two hours, then thirty minutes, and maybe four hours after that. Since babies need help falling asleep, it's up to us to make that happen.

As parents, we don't get the quality, deep sleep our bodies need. So even though you clock in eight hours a day, you still woke up several times. You don't get a chance to transition into deep sleep when you're only asleep two hours at a time.

Because sleep is such a hot topic, this chapter covers a lot. We'll talk about:

- How to get your twins to sleep
- Strategies to use when your twins won't nap
- What to do when they'll only sleep in your arms
- How to stay calm when your twins won't sleep

How to get your twins to sleep

You'd think all you need to do is put a baby down in his crib and he'll fall asleep right away.

Sure, sometimes that happens. More common, though, are babies who need the right environment and cues to fall asleep. Since they've been in your womb for months, this can get a little tricky. Below are sleep arrangements to get your twins to sleep:

- **Wrap them in a swaddle or blanket.** Many babies prefer the snug comfort of a swaddle or blanket. A swaddle also prevents their arms from hitting them on the face (a reflex they'll outgrow).

- **Lay your twins on their backs.** Your babies might resist sleeping on their backs because they've grown used to the fetal position, but sleeping on their tummies poses too many risks, no matter how much it seems they prefer it.

- **Put them to sleep in small spaces.** Many babies prefer the close comforts of bassinets, swings and other small-space sleeping arrangements. A crib can seem too wide and large when they were so used to the tightness of your womb.

- **Keep the room dark.** I'm a fan of darkening curtains hung in the room they'll be sleeping in, especially for nighttime sleep. These keep all lights outside from peeking in.

  Typical advice also says to put your twins to nap in bright rooms, and I don't always agree with this. The idea is to encourage your twins to differentiate between day and night. It's harder for them to sleep longer stretches during the day when the room is bright.

  But I think it's fine to draw the curtains and keep the room dark during daytime naps. Because even the darkest curtains won't keep daytime sunlight out completely. Compare the room at 12pm and 12am and the daytime will never be pitch black.

  I'd rather your twins sleep well for naps, even if it means longer stretches. If they're sleeping too much (which can happen), then you can draw the curtains and wake them up, but there's no point in making falling asleep even more challenging for your twins.

- **Together or apart?** This is up to you and your twins. See how well your twins respond to sleeping close together. Coming home from the hospital, they might do well sleeping right next to each other. They've grown used to having one another close by.

  In other cases, their cries might disturb one another and wake each other up. See how they fare, and you might end up switching sleeping arrangements back and forth.

Sometimes I'd put my twins together to nap in the Pack 'N Play or swaddled right next to each other on a blanket. Other times, I had to keep them far apart from each other because their cries would wake each other up.

- **Use different sleeping arrangements.** We'll talk about what to do when your twins won't nap below, but for now, think of different sleeping arrangements for your twins. They might nap in the bassinet for the first nap but won't sleep in it for the next.

  In that case, you might try wearing one baby in a wrap or carrier while the other is in the sling, or you might take both of them out on a stroll, or you might place one over your chest while the other sleeps in the crib.

5 best practices for establishing good sleep habits

It's never too early to establish good sleep habits in babies. Here are five important lessons to remember:

#1: Put your babies down drowsy but awake.

If you don't always want to be the only one who can put your twins to sleep, put them down drowsy but awake.

Rocking or nursing a baby to complete sleep means they don't have an opportunity to fall asleep on their own. They won't learn that they can suck on their hands, or rock their heads side to side, or coo, or find a position they like.

Put your babies down when they're drowsy and sleepy, but not completely asleep so they're just about ready but can take it from there on their own.

This may not always work. Sometimes you're better off putting a completely asleep baby down to save your sanity, but don't make that your go-to move. With each nap or bedtime attempt, try to put them down before they've fallen asleep.

#2: Give your twins a chance to lie awake.

We seem to think babies should fall asleep—and stay asleep—the minute we set them down. So a typical scenario usually involves mom holding a drowsy baby in her arms and setting him down, but the baby realizes he's in the crib instead of her arms. He doesn't look drowsy anymore and his eyes are wide open.

And what does mom do? She picks him up and rocks him back to a sleepy state. *Maybe THIS time it'll work*, she might think.

It may or may not, but you may not always have the time or ability to rock them to a drowsy state each time they're startled awake. So here's the secret:

It's totally okay for your babies to lie awake.

It really is. I had to come to terms with this. I thought my babies wouldn't sleep if their eyes were open after I put them down.

But think about your own sleep patterns. I'm sure there are nights it took you a few minutes to fall asleep after laying in bed. You may have even kept your eyes open before finally drifting off.

Being okay with your twins awake when you lay them down takes the pressure off your shoulders. You won't feel terrible because you have to rock or nurse them to sleep over and over.

That time laying on their backs can give your twins a chance to fall sleep on their own.

#3: Newborns can only stay awake for an hour to an hour and a half at most.

Remember how we said newborns sleep 16 to 17 hours a day? With frequent naps throughout the day, that means awake times are just as short.

Keeping your twins awake more than an hour and a half will overtire them, which doesn't lead to better sleep. They'll feel cranky and too tired to sleep well.

As we talked about with routines, this is one of the times when I recommend watching the clock. Don't put your twins down according to a set time (for instance, they must always take a nap at 3pm).

But do watch the clock to see how long they've been awake since their last nap. If it's been an hour, look for sleepy cues, depending on your babies' temperaments. If it's been an hour and a half, try to put them down for another nap.

#4: Have an early bedtime.

According to the fantastic sleep book, *The Sleepeasy Solution*, ALL children should be asleep by 8:30pm.

Even though newborns seem to sleep at all times of the day, aim to have an early bedtime. Unlike naps, bedtime usually involves an elaborate routine and settling in for the night. You might give them a bath beforehand, or read several books, or feed them to sleep (whereas during the day, you had been feeding them after waking up).

An early bedtime establishes good sleep habits they'll carry with them throughout childhood. They're also adjusting their internal clocks so they get used to long stretches of sleep at night. An early bedtime gives you a chance to sleep as much as you can (or tend to tasks before you head to sleep yourself).

#5: Sync your twins' sleep.

You'll drive yourself crazy if you try to maintain two different schedules for each twin. It's important to keep your twins' sleep the same.

How does this work, exactly? Through compromise.

Let's say you want both twins to sleep for two hours, from 12pm to 2pm. Except by 12:30pm, Baby A is already awake. Baby B, meanwhile, looks like he can keep sleeping until 2pm, or even longer.

Instead of waking Baby A up at 12:30 and leaving Baby B to sleep, compromise.

Check on Baby A to make sure he doesn't have a soiled diaper. Then encourage him to keep sleeping at least until 1pm.

Even if he doesn't fall asleep, at least you're giving Baby B a chance to keep sleeping. You're also letting Baby A know that it's still time to sleep, not be awake.

If Baby A still won't sleep by 1pm, then wake Baby B from his nap. Now, both babies will be up by 1pm.

Here's another scenario: let's say Baby A skipped the nap completely. He didn't even fall asleep until 12:30. Wake both twins at the same time, let's say 1pm.

Then, since they're younger than six months old, put them down for their next nap one hour from their wake-up time. Their wake -up time was at 1pm, so you'd put them down to nap at 2pm.

Yes, this means that Baby A will be awake for two hours, but that also means Baby B has only been awake for one hour. Both babies will compromise and meet each other halfway so that they can more or less be on the same schedule.

Your twins' schedules might look similar or different depending on their temperaments, but try to keep them on the same schedule so you're not tracking two different routines.

(Note: If they're six months or older, you'd put them down for a nap at their next designated nap time, not an hour from when you got them up.)

Strategies to use when your twins won't nap

There will come a time when your twins won't nap. Maybe they skip the entire nap, or wake up 10 minutes after you had just put them down. It's best to come prepared with strategies on what to do when that happens.

Look for sleep cues

The trouble with sleep is there's a window of opportunity for it to happen. Try to put them down when they're not tired, and it just won't work, but keeping them awake too long makes them too overtired to sleep well.

Watch the clock to see whether your twins will be getting sleepy any time soon. An hour to an hour and a half awake is about all a newborn can take before he's tired again.

Once you know the general time frame, look for sleep cues. Your twins might seem disinterested or overstimulated. They'll yawn. They'll root for something to suck, or even fuss. The easier you can spot their sleep cues, the more they likely need a nap.

Use routines for a smooth transition

By now, you know how important a routine is for your twins. Not only do routines signal to them that it's time for sleep, it also transitions them better.

Imagine playing on a mat or with a rattle, then being scooped up and placed in a crib. Pretty disjointed, right?

Instead, rely on your routines to make sure your twins get as much help as possible with going to sleep. The routine allows for enough time between their previous activity and sleep time.

Another thing: even if it's not part of your routine, keep activities subdued if you know nap time is coming up. Speak quietly, keep the room dark, put away loud toys. Little things to signal that it's wind down time.

Make the room conducive for sleep

If your twins sleep too long, then yes, put them to sleep in the middle of the living room with noise and bright lights, but if you struggle with putting and keeping your twins to sleep, then make the room conducive for doing so.

An environment for sleep can include:

- White noise, such as a fan, heater, or white noise machine
- Dark room
- Minimal distractions (like a mobile) or noise
- The right room temperature
- Comfortable clothes
- Comfortable sleeping area

Don't pick them up right away

No newborn should be left to cry with the intention of crying as a means to fall asleep.

But if you're washing bottles and you hear a baby, don't feel like you have to drop everything to pick her up right that instant. Finish washing the bottle, then calmly walk in and comfort her. Rushing to pick her up makes you more stressed, which only makes your twins feel the same.

More importantly, not rushing in will let your twins know it's okay to wait. By default, your twins will have to wait. There will be many times when you're putting one baby to sleep and you hear the other one crying. Once you're able to get to the crying baby, soothe and thank them for waiting and letting you finish what you had to do.

Figure out how much sleep your twins really need

A few months down the line, your twins will begin to drop naps. The struggle to put them down to sleep is actually their bodies saying they don't need to nap any longer.

If your twins regularly skip a nap for five consecutive days, it may be time to drop that nap. Rearrange your other naps so they allow for longer awake times in between. Fewer naps can mean better sleep because your twins will be needing less and less of it as they grow.

When they'll only sleep in your arms

Once you bring your twins home, you'll learn how much they enjoy sleeping in your arms. It's comfortable, familiar, and conducive for sleep. They'll probably sleep long stretches in your arms but skip their naps anywhere else.

This is all fine if you enjoy and have the time to hold your twins to sleep. Problem is, after a while, you might end up alone with both of them. Even with two adults, you might need or want to do something else, from chores to going to the bathroom.

What do you do when your twins have grown so used to sleeping in your arms that they won't sleep anywhere else?

Keep them snug

Your arms are so comfortable because they resemble the position and warmth of how it felt in your womb. If laying your twins flat on their backs in a crib won't work, try other ways to mimic the feel of your arms.

You might want to swaddle them to contain their arms. Sleep suits work well to give the all-around snugness throughout their bodies, and infant cushions like the Snuggle Me Organic adjusts to your baby's weight to mimic sleeping in arms.

Use sleep aids

During the newborn stage, sleep aids will come in handy when you're in pure survival mode. Long-term, these strategies won't work because babies can't reinsert pacifiers in their mouths as much as we wish they could, but in the meantime, they can mean all the difference between sleeping in your arms and not sleeping at all.

Try sleep aids like pacifiers or white noise machines like the Baby Shusher twin moms swear by. Darkening curtains keep the light outside from coming in, and baby gear like swings help lull them to sleep.

Put them in different sleeping arrangements

Putting my twins to sleep felt like a big game. When one tactic didn't work, I'd try another until it did. If you can't hold your twins and they refuse to nap in the crib, try different sleeping arrangements. Below are several potential places your twins can take a nap:

- Swing
- Bassinet
- Crib
- Taking them out in the stroller
- Baby wrap or carrier
- Baby bounce chairs
- On a blanket on the floor

How to stay calm when your twins won't sleep

The biggest frustration for many twin parents is when their babies won't sleep. Whether it's refusing to nap or waking up many times a night, sleep deprivation takes its toll.

I'll tell you right now that you'll lose your temper and get frustrated. It might be in the middle of the night when your twins jolt you awake right when you were about to sleep, or when you've rocked your twins over and over for naps that they still won't take.

Take heart: you're not alone. You're not a bad mom either for feeling frustrated or saying things you regret or didn't mean. We can't think clearly when we're sleep-deprived, and when you're running on no sleep for months, it gets to you.

But ideally, we'd all respond calmly and with compassion when our twins won't sleep. Even though we can't avoid frustration, being aware is the most effective way to remain calm. Just knowing and seeing yourself feel upset can make a huge difference.

So, how can you keep calm when your twins won't nap?

Change your environment

We sometimes do silly things, like repeating the same things even if they didn't work the first time. Imagine rocking your twins, settling them down, and they're wide awake. What do we do? Pick them up, rock them again, repeat.

Instead of repeating the same thing, change your environment. If putting them down in their crib won't work, try a different sleep arrangement. Put them down in a different part of the room, or even take a walk outside in the stroller. They'll likely sleep (or at least calm down) with a different environment.

Take a break

Feeling frustrated won't do you or your twins any good. They'll sense your frustration, feel stressed, and be less likely to fall asleep. Imagine trying to sleep with someone hovering above you, upset. Not exactly relaxing.

Instead, take a break. Maybe this means counting 60 seconds to clear your head. Walking to the bathroom to splash water on your face. Listening to a relaxing or even upbeat song to get you out of your funk.

Focus on your mental state first before succumbing to the frustrations. A quick break can be all you need to reset, rethink, and get a better handle on the situation.

Have company

Even if you're fine showing your true colors with friends and family, having company can calm you down.

That person can be the much-needed distraction or support to get you through a tough time. You're less likely to lose your temper if you know someone is there to witness it.

Make a list of your "go-to strategies"

Remember how I mentioned doing the same things over and over instead of changing it up? Part of the problem is we don't always know what to do, even if we know we should do something different.

When I had my twins, I taped a list of my "go-to moves" on several walls around my home. I referred to these lists when they were crying and fussy. It's too easy to feel desperate or hopeless when they cry, but if you have a list of go-to moves, you know exactly what methods you can try.

Accept it

I've learned the power of acceptance when it comes to overcoming feelings of frustration. Accepting that this is difficult can make a big difference in your mood.

To be clear, accepting your scenario isn't a sign of defeat. You're not saying, "Well, I guess I just have fussy babies and there's nothing I can do about it."

Instead, acceptance is being with your emotions and current state. You can still try to change and help your twins fall asleep or stop crying, but you're not beating yourself up if they don't.

After all, this is the season of your life. It will be hard. Anything different isn't realistic. You'll face tough times, but own your emotions. Don't try to deny your frustration, or feel guilty because you got mad. Notice it, and accept it. "It is what it is," as they say.

BREASTFEEDING
AND PUMPING

Breastfeeding, formula-feeding, exclusively pumping… which one is right for you?

Twin moms need to be flexible with our options. You may have well-meaning goals, but circumstances can change quickly.

I exclusively breastfed my eldest and expected to do the same with the twins, but even from the hospital, baby B was underweight. We were even running the risk of him having to stay at the NICU until he could pack on some pounds. Without hesitation, I chose to supplement with formula, knowing it would help him gain the weight he needed.

And thankfully he did.

For the first few months, I mostly breastfed the twins, but I also offered them formula from time to time. When I came down with thrush, I increased formula for both of them about 50% of the time.

Other moms might have imagined nursing from day one, but an unexpected complication with feeding means they're pumping breast milk instead, or they may have made up their minds to bottle-feed, but at the last minute decide to try breastfeeding. Anything can change with twins.

If you think breastfeeding twins seems daunting, you're not alone. Many have expressed how they want to breastfeed while admitting they're not sure how. In this chapter, we'll talk about breastfeeding and pumping for twins. You'll learn about:

- Breastfeeding in the first few days and what to expect
- Correctly latching your twins
- Tandem feeding success (or feeding at the same time)
- Keeping your supply up and adding to a freezer stash
- Pumping best practices

Breastfeeding in the first few days

Many of the challenges with breastfeeding starts in the first few days. We're still learning how to latch, and our milk still hasn't come in. We're emotional from welcoming twins, and we're faced with the initial discomfort of breastfeeding.

What can you expect in the first few days so you can prepare?

Your twins will nurse on colostrum.

Little did I know that we don't produce typical breast milk for the first few days. Instead, our bodies produce colostrum, a yellow-colored type of milk. A few facts about colostrum:

- **Colostrum has a high concentration of nutrients in low volumes.** This is why, if you pump in the initial days, you'll barely get anything compared to later days. It's perfect for newborns, though, whose immature digestive systems can't handle a large amount of regular breast milk just yet but still need those nutrients.

- **Colostrum is a laxative.** This helps your babies pass their first bowel movements and rid their bodies of bilirubin. High levels of bilirubin are what cause jaundice.

- **Colostrum is high in antibodies,** boosting your newborns' immunity.

Your milk will come three to four days after giving birth

Toward the third or fourth day after giving birth, you might start panicking and think, *Why isn't my milk coming in?!* It's easy to feel helpless especially if you're doing all you can to help your twins gain weight.

But don't worry—it'll come in eventually. Your babies need the colostrum, so the days of not having regular breast milk are totally normal.

Your body will begin producing regular breast milk when your breasts feel engorged. You'll notice that the milk you express will look white and more liquid.

And remember how your breasts grew a cup size (or two) when you were pregnant? Expect to grow another cup size when you're breastfeeding.

Breast milk comes in two stages.

When your twins begin a feeding session, the milk that comes out is called fore milk. It's lighter in color and has lower fat. After several minutes, the hind milk kicks in, which is creamier, whiter, and higher in fat.

Fore milk quenches your twins' thirst, while hind milk provides the nutrients. If you pump, you'll notice the bottles fill up with a lighter fore milk before the hind milk comes.

When you nurse your twins, try to have them drain each breast so they get both fore and hind milk.

Breastfeeding might be uncomfortable at first

I struggled with breastfeeding the first month, and that was with my eldest, not my twins. It hurt, I got blisters, and I was ready to quit each day.

Even with the correct latch, you might still feel discomfort during the first days, but after a while, your nipples "toughen up." You feel more confident, and you're able to latch the twins much better.

The strange thing? When I breastfed my twins, I felt zero pain. Just when I was anticipating another round of pain and discomfort, I felt none. Almost like I picked up right where I left off. My body wasn't any different than when I first tried breastfeeding my eldest.

So even if you hear from others about their initial pain, it's not guaranteed you'll feel any of it.

How to correctly latch your twins

I mentioned many times the importance of latching your twins correctly, so how exactly do you do that? These are the most important pointers to remember when latching your twins:

1. **Squirt a little bit of breast milk over the nipple.** Simply pinch the nipple until some colostrum or breast milk comes out through the ducts. The extra breast milk helps protect your nipples and is a familiar taste to your babies.

2. **Make sure your twins' tummies are facing yours.** What you don't want to see is your twins lying flat on their backs and their heads turned sideways toward you.

3. **Aim your nipple toward their upper lips and noses**, not the centers of their mouths.

4. **Wait for them to open their mouths wide.** Their mouths should cover the entire aerola, or the dark-colored area of your breast. If their mouths and lips are only covering the nipple, then they're latching incorrectly and it'll hurt. If they're not opening their mouths wide enough, don't force their mouths open with your breasts. Instead, tickle their mouths with your nipples until they open wide.

5. Once they're latched and sucking, **make sure their heads are tilted back.** You want space for them to swallow and breathe comfortably. What you don't want is their chin pressed on their chest. Try this yourself and you can feel how uncomfortable it would be to breathe or drink.

6. **Their lips should be splayed outward**, not tucked in. You should also be able to see their tongues if you pulled down on their lower lips.

7. Once they're done, don't just pull them off the breast. This will hurt since they've still got a suction on. Instead, **insert your pinky inside their mouths between their lips and breasts to break that suction**. You're adding air between the lips and breasts, making it more comfortable for you to unlatch.

Tandem feeding success

Besides latching correctly, another skill I'd encourage you to learn is tandem feeding. Nursing your twins at the same time will be one of the biggest ways to save time and hassle, but if the thought of nursing two at the same time has you confused, don't worry. We'll walk through the exact process of how to set this up.

Before we start, I suggest you get a nursing pillow before your twins arrive. Then, bring this with you to the hospital so you can practice right away.

I made the mistake of assuming I wouldn't need one or that I'd rely on regular sleeping pillows. A nursing pillow makes a huge difference. I used the My Brest Friend pillow for twins and loved how sturdy the pillow was. Once my twins were a little older and I was more confident, I could nurse them hands-free.

Another fantastic pillow other moms recommend is the Twin Z pillow. The texture is softer, so this can also double as a resting pillow when you alternate burping. The Twin Z pillow is also useful if you plan to bottle-feed, and it offers you back support.

How to get your twins into tandem feeding position

A typical tandem feeding position includes you sitting cross-legged on the bed or couch. You wear your nursing pillow around your waist. Each twin is in a football hold—their heads toward your breasts and their feet to your back. Then...

1. Get your twins on either side of where you plan to sit. That could be on your bed, the couch, or the floor. Lay them down in the position they'd be once they're on the pillow, so heads facing forward and feet facing back.

2. Wear your nursing pillow and sit in between your twins.

3. Pick one twin up first and lay him on the nursing pillow, football-hold-style. Make sure he has a good latch on your breast.

4. Once he's secure and nursing, pick up your other twin and latch him on.

In the first few days or weeks, try to have someone help you with tandem nursing. It can be overwhelming to manage on your own, so get your partner or family to help you nurse.

In that case, you'd sit with your nursing pillow, and someone can hand each baby to you.

How to burp your twins after tandem feeding

Burping two babies can be tricky. If other adults are with you, ask them to burp one baby while you hold the other. During the early weeks, you might have people visiting who can help. Your partner can burp one baby after middle-of-the-night feedings.

But if you're alone, you can still burp both twins after tandem feeding:

1. Once the twins finish nursing, unlatch both babies.

2. Then, carry one baby over your shoulder and pat his back for about a minute.

3. Set him back down on the pillow and repeat with the other twin.

At this point, you could either:

- keep the the nursing pillow around your waist and lay the waiting twin down near you (he'll still be at an incline), or

- lay both babies down, set the nursing pillow in front of you, and recline the waiting twin on it.

What you want to avoid is laying your babies flat on their backs after they just ate.

When I first breastfed my babies, I chose to nurse one at a time. I tried tandem nursing once at the hospital and felt too scared to do it again.

But here's a word of encouragement I wish I told myself. Even if it feels awkward, try tandem feeding at least once a day. Choose the best time when you're not sleep-deprived to practice (basically, not the middle of the night), and do it when someone can help. The quicker you can master tandem feeding, even for newborns, the more time you'll have.

Pumping best practices

Many moms who breastfeed also pump milk. Some return to

work and would still like to be able to provide their twins with breast milk. Others need a meaningful break from the baby, and pumping allows others to feed the baby in the meantime. Some might want to pump if their babies are in the NICU, and still others pump to increase supply (more on that below).

What are some of the best practices for pumping?

- **Use a hospital grade pump.** A pump can never be as efficient as a nursing baby, but if you had to choose one, go with a hospital grade pump. I used the Medela Symphony. These are pricey to own, so I suggest renting them either from your hospital or a local breastfeeding store.

- **Start pumping at the hospital.** Doing so stimulates milk production and sets you on the right track. You might only get a little bit of colostrum, but pumping plus nursing will signal to your body to produce milk.

- **Have an extra set of pump parts.** Even if you'll eventually have to wash all those pump parts, at least you have the option not to at that moment. Sometimes it's easier to stash your pump parts in the fridge and wash them in the morning. Knowing you have an extra set ready to go before the morning allows for that to happen.

- **Keep several of the white membranes handy** if you happen to use Medela. These can tear easily, and a broken piece means you'd have to run to your nearest store for a new pair. Save yourself the time and have a box both at home and at work.

- **Get a hands-free bra.** Like the nursing pillow, I didn't get a hands-free bra until much later. It was a hassle and affected my position. Once I got a hands-free bra, pumping became much easier.

- **Store breast milk properly.** Breast milk can remain in room temperature for up to four hours. In the refrigerator, bottles and bags of breast milk can be stored for three to five days. Frozen breast milk is best used within six months (but once it's thawed, don't re-freeze it).

- **Thaw frozen breast milk properly.** Don't thaw breast milk in the microwave or on the stove top too quickly (it doesn't heat through properly and some parts might be too hot). Instead, put it in the refrigerator the night before, or let it thaw in a bowl of warm water.

To exclusively pump or not?

A few moms choose to exclusively pump to give their babies breast milk without nursing on the breast. The most common reason is pain. Either the baby can't latch, or the pain is just too much for mom to handle.

I know several moms who chose this route, and they'll admit it's not an easy one. Exclusively pumping seems like an option if you feel scared or awkward about breastfeeding, but pumping all the time is a hassle and a huge time suck.

Not only do you need to take time away to pump, you also need to spend more time feeding the pumped milk to your babies. Even if you pump and your partner feeds, that still takes extra time than if you nursed.

This is true for any pumping scenario, such as pumping so you can get a break. You put in twice the effort (pumping and bottle-feeding) for the same result (getting your twins fed). So you can imagine how much more time consuming exclusively pumping can be.

If you decide to exclusively pump, remind yourself the reasons you're doing it to stay motivated. Also, allow yourself the kind of lifestyle where you *can* take your time. Maybe this is leading a less harried life, or having someone bottle feed or be with the twins while you pump.

How to increase and keep your supply up

Once you've got breastfeeding going, the next question is, *How can I keep my supply up?* This can be frustrating if you're not producing a lot, or would like to produce more than the amount you currently are. You might even want to build a large supply of milk before going back to work.

What are some ways to increase and keep your supply up?

Eat enough healthy food and stay hydrated

By far, a well-balanced diet and drinking enough water will help keep your supply up. Make sure you're consuming at least 1,000 *extra* calories a day—500 for each baby.

And just as you did when you were pregnant, drink plenty of water. You are what you eat, after all, including your breast milk. Your body can't produce if you're not consuming enough.

Pump in addition to nursing

Increase your supply through pumping—this tricks your body into producing more. A few ideas that have worked for many twin moms:

- **Option 1:** Pump 15 minutes after each feed, or at least the ones during the day. Your initial results may only be one ounce at most, but over time, you may be able to pump an extra five ounces!

- **Option 2:** Pump one hour after every feed, especially if your twins are on an every-three-hours schedule (as is typical in many NICUs). You're able to squeeze out extra ounces but with enough time for your breasts to produce more by the time your twins nurse.

- **Option 3:** If you've weaned from middle-of-the-night feedings, continue to pump. This will happen once your twins are older, but it's another way to trick your body to continue producing milk. Let's say your twins normally wake up twice a night, but you've been able to successfully wean them down to once or even none. You could still wake up, even just once a night, to pump.

As with anything in parenthood, keep a healthy balance of your goals with your needs. Unless you have a specific goal in mind (building up x amount of ounces before work), don't force yourself to pump when you don't have to. You'll feel better rested, happier, and healthier with extra sleep than extra ounces.

FORMULA
AND BOTTLE-FEEDING

There are two ways newborns can consume calories: breastfeeding and formula. Purees, regular milk, even water—those are foods to consume several months from now. This chapter focuses on everything formula-feeding and bottle-feeding (useful if you're pumping!). We'll cover:

* Different kinds of formula (and which one's right for you)
* Formula-feeding best practices
* How to bottle-feed twins at the same time

Different kinds of formula

Despite many brands of formula, you'll typically find two types:

* Ready-to-use
* Powdered

Ready-to-use formula comes in portioned, pre-filled bottles with sterilized nipples. You'll need to throw the bottle and nipple away after each use. These are the most convenient since everything is already portioned and ready to go with no need to wash later. These are also the more expensive option, and you can't portion the exact amount you want.

Powdered formula comes in tubs which you'll use to mix your own bottle each feeding. This type of formula is less expensive and allows you to measure exactly how many ounces you want in a bottle. It's also more inconvenient since you need to mix the powder with water in your own bottles (not to mention wash them later).

Both serve their own unique purposes. Ready-to-use formula makes for convenient travel or easier middle-of-the-night feedings. Powdered formula cuts down on costs and lets you better control the amount to offer your twins.

Formula-feeding best practices

Whether you only offer formula or use it to supplement, formula-feeding has its own best practices.

- For powdered formula, **use sterilized water**. I bought one-gallon jugs of water specifically for babies (you can find these in the baby aisle at the grocery store).

- Unlike breast milk, **don't freeze formula**.

- Powdered formula can typically be pre-mixed with water and stored in the refrigerator. For instance, you can prepare bottles in the morning for the rest of the day, but you'll want to **toss any unused bottles after 24 hours**.

- If your twins drank from a bottle of formula but didn't finish it, it's best to **toss it out to avoid bacteria** build-up. Each formula brand has its own specific storage and re-uses, but to be safe, don't save unused mixed formula.

- **Check your formula brand's instructions**. It'll have specific guidelines on how long bottles can be stored and how long they can be refrigerated or left at room temperature.

- **Always throw away expired formula**, even if it hasn't been mixed or opened.

- **Don't allow your twins to go to bed with a bottle**, no matter their age. Sleeping with a bottle damages their teeth and sets bad sleeping habits.

What kind of bottles and nipples to get?

Experiment with different bottles and nipples. Those that allow for air to pass are your best options. Old school glass bottles make babies suck extra air, which leads to gas and tummy troubles.

Instead, choose bottles like Playtex Ventaire or Dr. Brown's. These have more parts which can be annoying to clean, but they're designed to reduce sucking gas.

Wide bottles and nipples are also a good option for newborns. They're smaller so they're more compact, and wider to resemble a mother's breast.

Experiment with clear (silicone) and brown (latex) nipples as well. If you find your twins struggle with one, try the other. Our pediatrician told us newborns tend to prefer latex in the beginning, and most brands also offer nipples in levels for different ages.

How to bottle-feed twins at the same time

Now that you know more about the tools you need, let's talk about feeding twins at the same time. You have a few options to try:

Ask another adult to help feed

Your easiest option is to ask another adult to feed one twin while you feed the other. This is by far the biggest perks of bottle-feeding. Unlike tandem breastfeeding, they don't need you to eat!

Use a nursing pillow

Some nursing pillows like the Twin Z or even two Boppies allow you to rest your twins in them while you hold the bottles. During the newborn stage, you might want to add support with rolled up swaddle blankets on either side of each baby.

Sit cross-legged and place one twin on each leg

Place your twins on either side of you. Then sit cross-legged and place Baby A's head on your knee, then repeat with Baby B on the other knee. Another option is to sit with the soles of your feet pressed together and lay them the same.

Use infant seats and bouncy chairs

Once your twins are older and can hold their heads up, infant seats and bouncy chairs can be useful. This was the way our nanny fed our twins when she was alone with them.

COPING WITH
SLEEP DEPRIVATION

You've heard the horror stories. Maybe you already have other children and shiver with memories of those early days. Lack of sleep makes even the most patient mom irritable, disoriented, and downright tired. Now double that with twins.

What sleep deprivation with twins *really* feels like

So, what exactly does the sleep deprivation of twin parenthood look like? It's not like the all-nighter you pulled in college to study for an exam. Nor is it like the time (or two) you drank too much coffee and didn't sleep until 5am.

You see, in all those instances, you still had an opportunity to sleep after. Maybe you slept in the following day, or you took a day off from work to catch up. With twins, however, you're running on a serious lack of sleep, for months on end.

Worse, you don't get the quality of sleep you need. I clocked in a solid eight hours of sleep every day.., but spread out in chunks. I'd maybe sleep for an hour and 15 minutes here and two hours there, but it was never the deep sleep I needed. Even though I slept for eight hours a day, my body didn't feel like it. It's normal to be awake at least every hour and a half with your newborn twins. With two of them waking up throughout the night, you have less opportunity to fall and stay asleep.

Why babies wake up so often

So, why the frequent wake-ups? The biggest reason is your twins' need to eat. Their stomachs are tiny! On day one, their stomachs are the size of a cherry, with the capacity of about a teaspoon. By day three, it increases to the size of a walnut, or about one ounce. By one week, it's grown to the size of an apricot, about 1.5 to 2 ounces, and even that's not that big when you think about it.

Another reason babies wake up, usually around 90 minutes, is because of our sleep cycles. We all wake up many times throughout the night, but we know how to put ourselves back to sleep, but newborns don't. So they wake up, don't know how to fall asleep, and cry for us to help them figure it out.

And the reasons keep piling up. They feel hot or cold or wonder where they are when they wake up feeling disoriented.

As you might expect, the above applies to just one baby. Now imagine two, and you know why we twin moms are some of the strongest ones out there! But don't worry, because you'll manage, as we all have, sleep-deprived and everything. You'll learn some key strategies to help you get the most out of your sleep, even with twins.

To help you better manage sleep deprivation, let's talk about two issues here. First, we'll discuss several ways to help you better function during the day with little to no sleep. Second, you'll get tips on how to squeeze as much sleep as you can both during the day and at night.

How to function during the day with little to no sleep

Synchronize your twins (put them on the same schedule)

You might have heard the advice to put your twins "on the same schedule." I've said the same advice but have now changed it to "synchronize your twins." When you hear "putting twins on the same schedule," you assume it's doing things by the clock or at a certain time.

The newborn stage isn't conducive for putting your twins on a clock-based schedule. You can try in some cases—for instance, you can give your twins a bath at 6:30pm every night, but for most activities like eating and sleeping, wait on their cues or follow a flow instead.

So, what do synchronized twins look like? Do the same things for both twins.

If one twin wakes up to eat, feed both of them. If it's time to wake one up, wake the other. You'll have wiggle room, maybe 15 minutes here or half an hour there, but for the most part, you'll want to do the same activities for both twins. This saves you time from keeping track of who did what last time. You can also batch process many of your activities, such as feeding them or taking a nap while they both nap.

Conserve your energy

We forget that we tap into our energy resources throughout the day. Already running low on sleep, conserve your energy for when it matters. What does this mean?

Rest.

Combat sleep deprivation with its best antidote: sleep and rest. I remember trying to be several steps ahead, thinking I was saving time by doing it now instead of when I had to. On one hand, it's less stressful to prepare (we'll get into the benefits of being prepared soon), but otherwise, put aside most of your tasks, even if it's not "efficient," so you can rest instead.

Make sleep and rest a priority, and in many instances, your first one. Guard your chances to rest and take it seriously. Expect life to get chaotic and disgusting (think piled up dishes and unwashed hair), but rest assured that this is all temporary. Knowing it won't last forever means you can forgive yourself for not cleaning.

Find different ways to get the rest you need, as well. For instance, use disposable dishes and utensils for less washing. Ask friends and family to care for the twins or run errands so you can take a nap. Shop in bulk beforehand so you have all your household supplies stocked. You can be more efficient with your time and allot most of it to resting.

Track your twins' feedings and diaper changes

During the early weeks, you'll need to track your twins' eating and diaper changes to see how much they eat and how often. You'll also record whether they have wet and dirty diapers and what kind of poop they have.

Rather than trying to remember all these little details, write them down. You'll be foggy with sleep deprivation. The last thing you need is trying to remember which twin had a green poop and when you fed them last.

Whether you breastfeed or bottle-feed, record their eating and diaper changes.

Eat well and drink plenty of water

It's amazing how much what we eat and drink can affect our day. Downing a burger and soda can make you feel extra sluggish. Instead, as much as you can, eat healthier options. Homemade meals, even those pre-made from frozen dinners. Fruit and vegetable smoothies. Soups and salads. Not only will healthier food make you feel better, it'll also help you recuperate. Your body will be healing, so it's even more important to eat the right kinds of food.

If you can't—if the only thing you can eat is delivery pizza— that's okay, too. We're talking about the newborn days here, so we can't always be picky with what we eat. You may not have the option to eat healthy, but the more nutritious your choices, the better you'll feel.

And water! Don't forget to drink tons of water for all its benefits. You'll be more hydrated, avoid headaches, and make sure your body is performing as best as it can.

Take a walk

Once you're physically ready, try and take a walk outside. Feeling cooped up at home can weigh you down. A slow walk around the block can be all you need to feel refreshed or at least awake.

Start small. Maybe go on your own without the twins, even for a few minutes. Later, you can take the twins for a stroll with another adult.

My walks were my sanity-saving techniques, especially when I felt frustrated or helpless. I'd either get a quick break away from the twins, or I'd push them in the stroller. This would usually calm them down or at least give me something to do with them.

Come prepared

So here's the somewhat opposite side of the "Conserve your energy" tip. On one hand, you'll want to conserve your energy and rest as often as you can. Don't worry about the toys your toddler scattered on the floor or using paper plates so you have less to wash.

But you'll also want to prepare, especially when doing it last minute takes more time. For instance, middle-of-the-night wake-ups were not my best times. I was delirious, incoherent, and downright grumpy, and I knew I would already be feeling that way regardless.

So imagine how much more helpful it was to have everything I needed organized and within reach. I kept my nursing pillow, feeding tracker, and infant gas drops in the same place. I stocked the changing table with diapers and wipes so we weren't fumbling around in the dark. I also had my water bottle by my bedside table so I wouldn't have to go to the kitchen when I was thirsty. These are the things I prepared before going to bed, knowing I'd be in a worse mood without them.

For you, maybe it's washing your pump parts ahead of time so you always have a clean set ready to go, or packing your diaper bag the night before going to the doctor's office. Little things you can do that, if you were to put it off, would stress you out even more.

You don't want to get ahead of yourself, however, and prepare so much that you don't allow yourself to rest. Do enough to get through the next scenario, and give yourself the rest of the time to sleep and relax.

Laugh about it

There might be a time (or two) where you're so sleep-deprived you're almost looney about it. Instead of letting your problems weigh you down, laugh instead. It's more refreshing to laugh about yet another skipped nap than to grumble under your breath. Laughing keeps things in perspective.

Yes, it sucks to rock your twins for 45 minutes only for them to wake up the minute you put them down, but at the same time... it's just a nap. The more we can laugh about the absurdities of life with twins, the better we can cope.

Another aspect of laughing is to surround yourself with funny things. I'm talking movies, television shows, standup skits. Anything to watch or keep you entertained and remind you that there's life beyond twins. A life you'll go back to down the line.

As you can see, you can find ways to combat sleep deprivation. You won't get rid of it—even parents of singletons can't avoid it, but you can use smart strategies to cope as best you can.

Next, we'll talk about getting as much sleep as possible. We're not talking eight hours of uninterrupted sleep (though I do have a solution for that in the last tip), but ways to make it more conducive for you to sleep when the time calls for it.

How to get as much sleep as you can

Create a sleep environment

One of the most painful and annoying things about middle-of-the-night feedings is falling back asleep. Not only are you jostled awake by your twins' cries and hope they sleep soon, you now have to go back to sleep yourself. If your twins cried as as mine did, you'd have an hour and a half to do that before the same thing happened again.

With such a short window, create an environment conducive to sleep. Make your room pitch black, add white noise to muffle newborn baby sounds (it's crazy how those tiny sounds wake you up!), and make your bed. A comfortable, peaceful sleep environment makes falling asleep easier.

Ask for help

Many of us have friends and family ready to watch the twins, especially during those first few weeks. Don't turn down help! I know many parents prefer to spend the initial days as a family unit, away from others and building their bond, but with the challenge of twins, I encourage you to accept and ask for any help you can get. Even if you want to be alone, have others on stand by in case you reach a breaking point and realize you can use some help.

Remember too that help comes in many ways:

- Visitors can hold and watch the twins so you can nap, take a shower, or even get out of the house for a few minutes.

- Accept any gifts such as food or baby supplies.

- Visitors can help clean your home, cook, or run quick errands so you can sleep.

- Friends and family can spend the night (or several nights) at your home. They can have night duties such as holding a fussy baby or changing diapers.

And consider hiring help as well. Night nurses to help during the sleep-deprived and challenging hours of the night. A babysitter to play with your older kids or help during the frenzy of the early evenings. A cleaning crew so you don't have to worry about the upkeep of your home. If it's within your budget, consider hiring if you don't have family and friends nearby.

I was lucky because our families live nearby, so we had a supply of food, help, and company during the first few weeks. My mom also slept over a few weeks, especially in the early days and again when my husband returned to work. These are the sanity-saving "it takes a village" tactics that makes all the difference.

Sleep early

Before I had kids, a typical bedtime was around midnight, 11pm if I slept "early." With a newborn, bedtime moved up waaaay earlier.

Remember those eight hours I mentioned I used to get in total? That was only possible because I slept early. Aim for an 8pm bedtime, both for you and the twins. It'll be dark and late enough at night for your twins to settle in. It'll also be good for you to establish a routine—yes, even this early—to get them used to sleeping at night.

And sleeping early gives you as much time as you can to add up those hours of sleep. Yes, they're broken up into chunks, and you're not getting that long stretch of deep sleep, but chunks of sleep are better than none.

With newborn twins, you won't get long hours to rest, but you should still consider yourself a patient as well as a mom. Your body is also healing, so you need to sleep as much as you can. Do the important tasks you can't neglect, then focus on napping throughout the day.

No caffeine close to bedtime

As much as you may love coffee or caffeine, begin to lay off the drinks after a certain time. Figure out your cut-off, and hold back on the coffee after that point. It's pretty hard trying to fall asleep when you're wired to stay awake.

I don't drink coffee so my body is pretty sensitive to the small amounts of caffeine I get from tea. I know that any caffeinated drinks I consume after 12pm will only spell trouble for me come bedtime.

Nap

One of the most common pieces of advice: nap when the baby naps. At first I thought this was ridiculous. *When else would I be able to [do this] or [do that]?!* I thought.

Yes, the times when your twins nap can be golden opportunities to do so many things. Clean, prepare, shower, run errands. Except I'm going to circle back to what I mentioned earlier about your priority. You'll have a few must-do tasks here and there, some which you can only do when the babies are sleeping, but for the most part, your priority (at least one of the top ones) should be to rest and sleep.

Imagine you had just left the hospital for another procedure, not for childbirth. Would you expect yourself to be up and about, cleaning, cooking and running errands? Probably not. More likely, you'd confine yourself to bed, resting the hours away.

You won't be stuck in perpetual sleep deprivation. When you're in the thick of it, remember—this too shall pass. I was the last person to ever believe this, both with my eldest as a first-time mom and again as a mom of twins. I couldn't fathom how this could improve at all, or imagine my life going back to normal. The good news is, it does. It'll take time, but with the right resources and frame of mind, you'll survive the sleep deprivation of newborn twins.

GOING OUT AND ABOUT
WITH TWINS ALONE

During the first few weeks with your twins, you'll likely be holed up at home resting with no agenda whatsoever. Eventually, that transitions to taking them out for a doctor's appointment, or a quick walk around the block. From there, you take a mighty leap: you go out with your twins for a fairly big errand... all on your own.

Yikes!

If that just made you panic a tad, you're not alone. I still remember driving to the library and realizing I didn't know how to unfold the darn stroller by myself. It can be overwhelming to handle twins on your own. Still, it's important to make that leap. Only in doing so do you build confidence. Plus, you're able to run errands, do something fun, and get out of a rut.

So, how do you get out and about with your infant twins alone?

Go to places you've been to

One of the easiest ways to be out with twins is to stick to places you're familiar with. Visit the local park you've always taken your other kids to. Go to the mall by your house, or the library you usually borrow books from.

The more familiar your surroundings, the less you'll need to adjust to on top of caring for your twins. You won't have to look up directions to get there or find the best place to park. You'll know exactly where to go and the hours they'll be open. Stick to familiar places to reduce the stress of coping with twins alone.

Use your double stroller

Your double stroller will be your second set of arms. I used that sucker just to get from the front door to the car. You're able to put both babies in one place and still free your arms to do other things. Who knows, your twins might even nap while you stroll.

Your stroller can act as a shopping cart or storage area, too. You may not be able to buy a week's worth of groceries, but you can hang bags on the handles or stuff your items in the storage area.

Come prepared

Do your twins have a favorite stuffed animal or biting ring? Bring those with you as emergency entertainment. I'm not a huge fan of distracting fussy kids, but sometimes you just need to get it done.

Bring pacifiers as well. One of my twins took to the pacifier more than the other, but both of them would at least give it a shot when they'd fuss.

Coming prepared also means packing a well-loaded diaper bag with extra clothes and diapers. Making sure they were fed before leaving. Going after a nap so they're not cranky, and keeping the length of your outing manageable.

Pick up one fussy baby at a time.

"What if both babies cry at the same time?!" That was my biggest fear of being out and about with twins. I didn't know what I'd do if both of them started crying.

The simplest solution: pick up one fussy baby at a time. It's totally okay to park the stroller and pick one up to calm and soothe.

I also rarely had to deal with two fussy babies at the same time. I had been imagining the worst, but for the most part, my twins took to their strolls. If anything, one baby would fuss while the other would remain calm, and I was able to focus on that one baby while the other waited.

When both babies would cry and picking them up one at a time didn't work, then I knew it was time to head home, but like I mentioned, those moments were rare. Don't be afraid to be out and about with twins because you're outnumbered, or worry about what others might think. I worried other moms would pity me, something I didn't need at that moment. Instead, I learned that moms are the most forgiving and understanding bunch (because we've all been there!).

Being alone with twins at home is hard enough. Being out with them ramps up the challenges you face. Here's the thing though. Difficult situations, including being out and about with twins, make you feel strong. You'll always wonder whether you can do it or not until you actually start. Start small, but start. You'll get the hang of it with every outing you take with your twins.

CONCLUSION

You made it through the book—congratulations!

You've learned how to manage your emotions and cope with a difficult pregnancy. You know how to prepare your family for this big change in your lives and how to prepare for them financially. You've learned how to balance work and twins and know exactly what you need for their arrival. You've developed an action plan for your delivery and know how to care for them when they arrive. Now you have the tools to best prepare for their arrival.

But you're not done yet. The arrival of your twins is just the beginning. With parenthood, the journey starts here. Your twins will challenge you in ways you never thought possible. Parenthood will test your limits. The beauty of it all? You'll realize just how strong, dedicated, and patient you are.

And remember, you are never alone. You have a community in our awesome Facebook group, All About Twins, to rely on. You have the knowledge you learned from this guide. You have the support to get you through even the toughest of days.

Congratulations on completing the book, and most of all, on the upcoming arrival of your twins!

xo,

Nina

YOUR FREE BONUSES

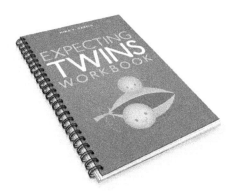

The Expecting Twins Workbook

I find it helpful to have printables, checklists, cheat sheets and all those goodies on hand to prompt me to taking action and staying organized. And so, along with the Expecting Twins Guide, I also created the Expecting Twins Workbook.

At 60+ pages, the workbook includes information not in the guide as well as supplemental sheets to tie in to the chapters.

All About Twins Facebook Group Membership

I don't want you to go through your twin pregnancy alone, or feel like you can't ask me or other twin parents questions you may have. I created a community so you'll always have a place to vent, ask, celebrate and talk all things twins.

Download your workbook and claim membership here:
sleepingshouldbeeasy.com/twins-workbook

ABOUT THE AUTHOR

Nina V. Garcia is a mom to three young boys. She started her blog, Sleeping Should Be Easy (sleepingshouldbeeasy.com), to record everything she was learning about being a mom. Her ebook, *How to Sleep Train Twins*, has helped hundreds of twin parents find the sleep they and their families need.

In addition to her blog, Nina's writing has been featured in other publications, including BlogHer, Scary Mommy, and The HerStories Project. She lives in Los Angeles.

CPSIA information can be obtained
at www.ICGtesting.com
Printed in the USA
LVHW081952270221
680129LV00038B/742

9 781542 426374